CALIFORNIA NATIVE GARDENING

California Native Gardening

A MONTH-BY-MONTH GUIDE

 HELEN POPPER

UNIVERSITY OF CALIFORNIA PRESS

Berkeley Los Angeles London

Contents

Introduction California Local

Gardening with natives means gardening with plants that have belonged for millennia in the place we call home. Natives reflect the characteristics of their locales. They survive on rainfall and the other water sources of their habitats. They are adapted to prevailing temperatures and to local, often distinctive, soils. Existing with one another, many of them share resources—even water—through interconnected underground root structures. They feed, shelter, and depend on native wildlife, including butterflies, birds, and other pollinators.

Tailored to where we garden, native plants offer us unsurpassed practicality. Compared with introduced plants, indigenous ones generally require fewer inputs. Locally adapted plants usually need less supplemental water, and few benefit much from fertilizer or amendments. They also typically require less work: less replanting, less protecting, and less pruning.

Echoing the wilderness, natives also give us something more. They bring habitat, and they bring a sense of place. Into a native garden comes the call of a quail, the revelry of cedar waxwings, the scurrying of a fence lizard. Into a native garden comes the surprise and delight of volunteer natives, some brought by birds from a distant park, others sprung from long-dormant seeds. From each native garden, a thread extends to the exquisite tapestry that defines our state.

◄ Oak leaves unfurl and lupines bloom in the Salinas Valley. JUDY KRAMER

OUR SIDE OF THE MOUNTAINS: CISMONTANE CALIFORNIA

California is large and diverse. What unites much of it for gardeners is a pattern of cool, wet winters and long, dry summers. The pattern reigns over all that lies between the Pacific Ocean and the seaward side of our highest mountains. From the lower reaches of western Oregon, through all of western and central California, into the northwest corner of Baja California, and encompassing the Channel Islands, this is the land known as cismontane California. Each winter, it receives the lion's share of water brought to these latitudes by North Pacific storms. Meaning "this side of the mountains," the appellation *cismontane* reminds us of the high mountain ridges to the east and south, which stall the Pacific storms and leave a different, more arid landscape beyond.

On our side of the mountains, we typically can rely on rain to water our gardens in winter, with occasional showers helping in fall and spring. Gardens green up during this relatively mild, wet season. When the rains cease in spring, we begin to recognize three distinct types of gardens: gardens where nature itself provides additional water, perhaps from fog, seeps, or streams; gardens that are regularly irrigated; and summer-dry gardens, with plants that demand little or no water in the dry season.

While some natives fit most naturally into the summer-dry garden, many of our signature natives fit in almost anywhere. Common perennials, such as monkeyflowers (*Mimulus* spp.) and California fuchsias (*Epilobium* spp.) make their way easily into gardens of all types. Across many habitats, gardeners emulate classic wildflower combinations, such as lupines with poppies (*Lupinus* spp. with *Eschscholzia californica*). Characteristic trees and shrubs, such as oaks, manzanitas, and ceanothus (*Quercus, Arctostaphylos,* and *Ceanothus* spp.), dot gardens in the foothills, in the chaparral, and in the Central Valley. The most ubiquitous natives take many forms, with distinct species and strains adapted to different locales. Across the wilderness, and from garden to garden, such familiar natives unify the mosaic of cismontane California.

THE PIECES OF THE MOSAIC

Up close, we see the individual pieces of the mosaic, and stark differences emerge. Some of us garden along the coast, under cool redwoods or amid the billowy shrubs and flowers of coastal scrub. Others garden in the Central Valley, once filled with the grasses and wildflowers of a California prairie. Still others garden in oak woodlands or where the tough shrubs of the chaparral once dominated the land. Across these settings, weather, soil, and terrain all differ. Every piece of the mosaic has its own mixture of plants, some common to all areas, some exclusively local, some altogether rare.

In each area, we see natives in the wild that are appropriate to our gardens, both practically and aesthetically. We borrow from nature's local compositions. A rhododendron (*Rhododendron macrophyllum*) blooms against the deep-green backdrop of huckleberry shrubs (*Vaccinium ovatum*) in the northern reaches of the redwoods. Sea pink (*Armeria maritima*) brightens rocky ledges near the shore. Inland, baby blue-eyes (*Nemophila menziesii*) lay a carpet under a valley oak. Cream cups (*Platystemon californicus*) and

Sea pink opens its blooms on the Mendocino coast.
JUDY KRAMER

3

goldfields (*Lasthenia californica*) cover a southern mountain meadow. Wherever we live, a distinctive beauty comes into focus. We recognize the face of home, and native gardening begins.

THE GARDEN'S RHYTHM

Baby blue-eyes, goldfields, and tidy-tips bloom under oaks in the Southern Coast Ranges. JUDY KRAMER

The type and timing of all of our gardening activities vary across these many locales. The summer pruning needs of redwood understory gardens differ from those of the chaparral. Spring arrives in February in some places and in May in others. Blended gardens spread out the timing. Each garden has its own pace.

Even for an individual gardener, activities shift from one year to the next, reflecting the gardener's fervor, the vagaries of weather, and the garden's continual change. Yet there is a rhythm to native gardening in California. It is the rhythm that makes gardening with natives so different from conventional gardening, and it is the rhythm that we native gardeners share on our side of the mountains.

The monthly chapters of this book follow the garden's rhythm. To mark the transition from one gardening year to another, the book begins with October, when cismontane California leaves the dry season behind and prepares for its own green "spring." As the year progresses, each month's chapter highlights the gardening tasks that many of us are likely to share.

While each chapter is meant to be read on its own, the precise timing of the tasks—of planting and pruning, of weeding and watering—will depend on each gardener's interest and needs. After leafing through the chapter on May, one gardener might skip ahead to the detailed watering section in June, while another might skip to the fire safety section in July. The chapters overlap, repeating some tasks and describing how others may differ from garden to garden or year to year.

As native gardeners, we observe both the rhythm and the changes each year. Our activities put us in the habit of noticing the details of our surroundings. Consciously or not, we hone a sense of place and a sense of time. Native gardening enriches us throughout the year, and this book is offered as a friendly companion along the way.

October

The dog days of summer are only just behind us, and the soil remains parched until the first rains descend. Weeks of warm air and blue skies fill much of October. While Labor Day inaugurates fall elsewhere, Halloween is the eve of autumn here.

For many of us, planting is the month's biggest and most satisfying garden chore. Native gardeners in the mild-winter areas, where most Californians live, await the first soaking rains to signal the start of the planting season. Gardeners in areas overrun with deer prepare plant cages for anything they cannot resist planting now.

For gardeners who plant in spring or who have mature gardens, clearing away damaged wood and watering are the key tasks. Pruning dead limbs is a job to be done before

‹ Lilac verbena comes from Cedros Island. With just a little water and occasional dead-heading, it provides fragrant blooms for months. SAXON HOLT

OCTOBER'S JOBS

Sow annual wildflowers

Rid the soil of weedy competition, water or wait for rain, then sow the seeds of California's colorful beauties.

Buy native plants

This is an ideal time to buy plants from native nurseries and plant sales for fall planting. If you have a place to shelter containers from weather and predation, you also can buy now for spring planting.

Begin to plant

For most of us, the planting season begins with the rains. Wait for soaking rains or prepare the site by watering deeply as soon as air temperatures cool.

Plant trees from seed

As soon as you begin to notice acorns on the ground, collect them from the trees themselves. Plant coast live oak (*Quercus agrifolia*) acorns soon after you collect them. Store other oak acorns in the refrigerator for a month before planting them. Start buckeyes (*Aesculus californica*), boxelders (*Acer negundo*), and California black walnuts (*Juglans californica*) from seed now.

Start cool-season grasses

Most of California's native grasses are cool-season ones. They are easy to establish in October.

Clean up

Wind is on its way; remove any damaged limbs that are vulnerable to it. Rejuvenate perennials by cutting back the remaining ones. Add or remove mulch as needed.

Water

Water new plantings and containers during dry spells, and water extra if those dry spells are windy. Once the cool days arrive, you also can water to nudge new fall growth along.

winds knock them down for us. Watering brings forward the fall growing season, and deep watering ahead of a dry Santa Ana wind protects vulnerable plants from desiccation.

Whether we plant, prune, or water this month, we all can enjoy the local native plant sales, and we all can take in the month's montage of color. Asters, sunflowers, and California fuchsias (*Aster* spp., *Helianthus annuus,* and *Epilobium* spp.) still bloom brightly, while cool-season grasses begin to freshen, toyon berries color up (*Heteromeles arbutifolia*), and the leaves of maples (*Acer* spp.) are touched with gold. In October's garden, summer mingles with autumnal change.

NATIVE GARDENING IN OCTOBER
Sow Annual Wildflowers

Sow California's spring-blooming annuals now, in fall. You can wait for the first soaking rains, or you can get a head start if you are willing to water. Some of the easiest and most arresting wildflowers are baby blue-eyes (*Nemophila menziesii*), bird's-eye gilias and globe gilias (*Gilia tricolor* and *G. capitata*), California poppies (*Eschscholzia californica*), and elegant clarkias and farewell to spring (*Clarkia unguiculata* and *C. amoena*). All are prized as much abroad as they are at home. Baby blue-eyes, clarkias, and poppies have been especially popular among the English, who have bred many clarkia and poppy selections. Globe gilias are popular with butterflies. Seeds of all of these annuals are widely available from specialty nurseries and sometimes even from big-box stores. In many locations, native specialists and local chapters of the native plant society are permitted to collect and sell the seeds of the locally native forms.

As easy as these native wildflowers are, they—like all wildflowers—have four key needs: the right location, relative freedom from weeds, protection from animals, and appropriate water. Many plants share these needs; but for annuals, the brevity of their lives, together with the fact that they typically are started in the garden from seed, makes them more exacting in their requirements. When their needs are met, annuals thrive and reseed themselves. If they are left to their own devices, the results will be as haphazard as the year's variation in the weather.

The right location provides adequate sun exposure, the preferred type of soil, and good drainage. Most of California's native wildflowers, including those above, need considerable sunlight. Notable exceptions include Chinese houses (*Collinsia heterophylla*) and red ribbons (*Clarkia concinna*), which grow in shade. While the easy germinators mentioned here are tolerant of most soil types, they do best in well-drained soils. (With good drainage, California poppies are perennials.) Some others, such as downingias (*Downingia pulchella, D. concolor,* and *D. cuspidata*) and meadowfoam (*Limnanthes douglasii*), are found in vernal pools and thrive in wet clay soils. For beautiful blooms, choose the right location.

Before wildflower seeds can be sown successfully in a new area of the garden, weeds should be allowed to germinate and then be removed. This requires some patience. The straightforward approach is to water the area as soon as the weather cools, and to continue to water until the weeds pop up. Then you can hoe them over and sow the wildflower seeds. Inevitably, some weeds will be missed, and you will want to follow up with more weeding later. If your sowing area is wide, you will have to decide whether the weeding is worth crushing a few seedlings along the way.

Consider sowing in drifts of a single species. While there are many wonderful native mixes available, single-species drifts make it easier to distinguish newly germinated wildflowers from weeds. They also help attract bees and butterflies, which often fly from flower to flower of the same species. Sow single species in drifts that are large enough—at least sixteen feet square—to be noticed by pollinators. That should bring in butterflies or native bees if they already visit your area. If such visitors are scarce, plant in still larger drifts so the pollinators will find your flowers.

To sow seeds evenly and help them come into contact with the soil, mix them into a handful or more of fine soil or sand before broadcasting them. If you have a few spare pots, sow some of the seeds in the pots and label them. The labeled pots will help you learn to recognize the seedlings, and they will provide something nice to give your friends in the spring. The pots do dry out more easily than the ground, so give them a little afternoon shade, and put them where they will be easy to water.

Once sown, the seeds need protection from birds, rodents, snails, and slugs. Some gardeners walk over the area to nudge their seeds into close contact with the soil. They then cover the soil with leaves or twigs and leave it at that. Others, relying on a technique popularized by the Theodore Payne Foundation, lay down pebbles before they sow. In the foundation's Fall 2008 newsletter, Dylan P. Hannon notes that "a light covering of gravel helps young plants flourish. A thin layer (one to two stones in thickness) of pebbles (about one centimeter in diameter) is sufficient." The seeds fall between the tiny rocks, which protect them from predation, weather, and movement. Still other gardeners use more substantial methods, such as covering the area with raised netting or row cover. When plundering is severe, or when the wildflower seeds are especially prized, ambitious gardeners sow in greenhouse flats and transplant the seedlings into the garden.

Appropriate water begins at sowing and continues throughout the life of annuals. Water gently at first, returning again and again with a fine mist so that you do not wash away the seeds or knock down the tiny seedlings. Ideally, you will have sown when rains are forecast, and you can leave it at that for a while; but rains are hit-and-miss everywhere in October and are absent altogether in some parts of the state. Water when it doesn't rain, and keep the soil moist when the air is dry and windy. As the winter rains fill in, so will the plants, and you will enjoy their fresh, glistening foliage as they make their way toward spring.

Buy Native Plants

In most of the state, natives are best planted in the fall, and native nurseries and botanic gardens anticipate gardeners' needs. So do the local chapters of the California Native Plant Society. From the North Coast to San Diego, local chapters hold their major plant sales in the fall, mostly in October. Experienced native gardeners and plant specialists preside, answering questions and guiding gardeners in their selections. They can help you choose the right plants for your garden conditions. While it is possible with great effort to modify your garden conditions, the easiest approach is to choose from among the plants that are native to your own area and that grow well in the conditions that already predominate in your garden. The Native Plant Society members at the plant sale can tell you which plants are native to the area and in what habitat they belong.

The members propagate many of the plants they sell from local selections or from cuttings from their own gardens. This makes their plants good bets for your own garden.

Conventional nurseries now carry natives as well, sometimes in a special section, sometimes mingled with the nonnatives. Typically, you can find several garden-friendly species of ceanothus (*Ceanothus* spp., also called California lilac) and manzanita (*Arctostaphylos* spp.), as well as nonwoody perennials, such as seaside daisy (*Erigeron glaucus*) and yarrow (*Achillea millefolium*). Many natives are not showy in containers, particularly in the fall, so nurseries are sometimes reluctant to carry large inventories of them. However, most are happy to order native plants for individual customers. Several wholesalers who handle natives list their inventories online. By looking at wholesalers' inventories, you can get a good idea of what is easily available for your retailer to order.

Do not be discouraged if a nursery staffer earnestly tries to steer you away from natives, suggesting that they are "difficult" to grow. This increasingly rare view usually comes from inexperience, or from the unfortunate experience of planting a native that needs summer dryness alongside an exotic that needs—and gets—summer water. Politely explain what you would like ordered, or seek out a more knowledgeable horticulturalist (sometimes the nursery's buyer or manager) to assist you. You are now a native gardening ambassador.

Native botanic gardens and native retail nurseries—both online and on the ground—have much wider selections, along with dedicated, knowledgeable staff. Their inventories include many plants that have been selected for good garden features, such as a long blooming period, striking foliage, or adaptability to irrigation. The staff members are experienced with native plants that work well in home gardens.

Habitat restoration nurseries also sell native plants. Some are open to the public, though usually for limited hours. Restoration nurseries sell plants in large quantities, usually in pots that home gardeners are not used to, such as "rose pots" or "tree bands." The pots are sometimes just two or three inches wide but are quite deep. Compared with traditional one-gallon containers, these narrow pots require less digging, but they demand more experienced, or more delicate, handling. Expect the staff to be more focused on habitat restoration than on gardening. Like the wholesale nurseries, many restoration nurseries post their inventories on their websites, and it can be helpful to study the list before you arrive. If you have a large area to cover, you know what you want, and they carry it, then a restoration nursery is a good choice.

CHOOSE THE RIGHT SIZE Wherever you decide to shop, buy plants that are appropriately sized for your garden. In our desire for an instant filled-in look, we can be tempted to choose large, fast-growing plants and crowd them together. That approach is expensive, requires extra work both now and later, and ultimately results in unhealthy plants and a less attractive garden. Instead, space large plants appropriately and fill in with annuals or low, fast-growing native perennials that are either short lived or easy to pull out later. Or just mulch between the young plants to keep down weeds, then revel in the luxury of space and enjoy the wait.

You should also buy plants that are appropriately sized for their containers. Don't be put off by a small plant in what might at first glance seem to be an overly large container. The roots are often larger than the plant, and they need space. Worse yet, don't be seduced by a big plant in a small pot. While plants in small containers usually cost less than those in large ones, a plant that is too large for its container is no bargain. It may have been "pushed" with too much fertilizer or it may be rootbound, a defect that many plants (woody ones in particular) will never overcome. When cost is the overriding concern, buy small plants in small containers, and console yourself with their ease of planting and with the knowledge that plants from small containers catch up quickly.

When you get the plants home, keep them in a place that is sheltered from the sun and easy to water until you are ready to plant them. Nursery containers dry out quickly and heat up fast, so even plants that will require full sun once they are in the ground should be protected from it in the meantime. You may also want to group plants by their eventual location. If you are not quite sure where you will situate them, then group them by their origin (chaparral, redwood, etc.) or cultural requirements (sun with

Container plants with similar requirements are grouped together while they await planting. These yarrow and coyote bush starts are destined for a rooftop. HELEN POPPER

good drainage, shade and regular water, etc.). Grouping the plants will help you sort out their eventual locations, and it will help you keep them healthy until you are ready to plant them.

Begin to Plant

For most of us in California, fall is the ideal planting time. With shortening days, cool air, and still-warm soil, plants direct their growth to their roots. If put in the ground now, they will have ample time to establish themselves before the trials of summer drought. Whether we wait for the first soaking rains or nudge our gardens along with supplemental water as soon as the weather cools, fall brings us out into the garden with our trowels and spades.

For other gardeners, deer and winter freezes make fall planting less than ideal. The lush young plants from the nursery entice the deer, and juvenile "deer-resistant" plants often lack the defenses that confer resistance later. Planting now requires the installation of fences or substantial plant cages. The head start on the roots may not be worth the headache of protection. In areas with hard winter freezes, there is no head start at all; spring planting is preferable.

Whether one plants now or waits for rain or spring, planting entails preparation, the planting itself, and immediate follow-up. Begin the preparation by choosing the locations that match the plants' needs and your desires. With plants already grouped by habitat, put them in the parts of the garden that suit them best. Locate chaparral shrubs, such as island bush poppies and woolly blue curls (*Dendromecon harfordii* and *Trichostema lanatum*), on a slope or in coarse, fast-draining soil. Put redwood understory perennials, such as Pacific bleeding hearts and swordferns (*Dicentra formosa* and *Polystichum munitum*), in shade and near a water source. Then, within these areas, give each individual plant enough space. If a shrub will grow to be six feet wide, center the planting hole at least a few feet from the mature plants around it, and even farther from other newly planted ones, which will grow larger. Finally, situate the plant to take advantage of the attributes you most admire. If the subtle, spicy scent of wax myrtle (*Myrica californica*) calls to you, plant it near a path, where you will release its fragrance as you brush against it from time to time. If you long for the old-fashioned delicacy of candied violets, plant mountain violets (*Viola purpurea*) where you can reach them easily, pick their flowers, and bring them into the kitchen.

Once you have decided where the plants will go, water both the plants and the sites well. Give them time to drain, then choose a cool day or time of day to begin digging the first planting hole. Push aside any mulch so it will not fall into the hole. Dig the holes substantially wider (as much as twice as wide) and a bit deeper than the plant's root ball or container. Scuff up the sides and bottom of the cavity, so the plant's roots eventually will be able to penetrate easily into the garden soil beyond. Scuffing is particularly important in clay soil, where a spade can leave behind a slick, impenetrable wall. Then build the bottom of the cavity back up again with the dug soil so that when the plant is placed in it, the base of the plant is raised slightly above the surrounding soil level.

Next, ease the plant out of the container. Loosen and unwind any coiled or turned-back roots. If untangling the roots leaves a hollow at the bottom of the root ball, then build up the center of the planting hole a bit more and spread the roots around it. Check to make sure the crown of the plant is high enough so that when you finish backfilling and tamping,

❮ Sharing cultural requirements, ferns and coral bells make good companions in a little grotto. HELEN POPPER

❯ This root ball will get only a slight detangling at its edge before being set into the ground. HELEN POPPER

it will be half an inch or so above the surrounding soil level. If the roots lie coiled at the bottom of the hole, then dig a little deeper so they have a chance to spread out. Backfill with the same soil you dug out, without fertilizers or other amendments. Be careful to keep mulch out of the hole, and try to fill it thoroughly so that there are no air pockets.

Next, using your feet, tamp down the soil around the plant to fill any leftover air pockets. Do this gently; overly vigorous tamping will crush the roots and compact the soil. Check the crown again to make sure that it is slightly above the surrounding soil. Most importantly, do not leave the crown in a depression, where water will stagnate, mulch will pile up, and fungal disease will thrive. Once the plant is well situated, finish by watering it thoroughly and mulching around it. Finally, remember that gardens change over time. As your native garden matures, you will move some plants, you will remove others, and you will plant again.

Plant Trees from Seed

Some gardeners start trees from seed and skip containers altogether. Mindful of the trees' ultimate dimensions and requirements, they sow seeds right where they want the trees to grow. Direct seeding entails losses, but it takes less work than planting from containers, and it costs much less. It also allows for excellent root development. Plant the big, ripe seeds of a buckeye (*Aesculus californica*) now. Or sow the seeds of a boxelder (*Acer negundo*) or a California black walnut (*Juglans californica*), or the acorns of a coast live oak (*Quercus agrifolia*). All are likely to catch up quickly with trees transplanted from containers.

Collect the acorns of blue oaks, black oaks, valley oaks, or Engelmann oaks (*Quercus douglasii, Q. kelloggii, Q. lobata,* or *Q. engelmannii*) when they just begin to drop from the trees. Collect the ones still in the trees; they are the healthy ones. Native Americans collect them by shaking the branches. You can do the same, letting them fall onto a tarp. Protect the acorns from drying out until you plant them. You can improve their germination by storing them in the refrigerator (that is, by using cold stratification). Remove their caps, soak the acorns, and toss away any that float. Some serious gardeners rinse the acorns in a dilute bleach solution—about half a cup of bleach in a gallon of water—to prevent mold. Finally, let them dry out briefly on towels or paper, and then store them in a freezer bag in the refrigerator. Remember that the acorns are alive; don't pack them in too tightly. If you notice a few germinating, plant those right away. Otherwise, keep them cool for a month before planting.

Once you have chosen the right locations for your trees, clear the planting areas of weeds, which can shade out young seedlings. To discourage early predation, some gardeners plant seeds in "collars." The collars can be made by removing the bottoms of cottage cheese containers and topping them with a cylinder of insect screen that is about eighteen inches tall. Or you can stake in a cylindrical cage of wire screen. If you do not use a collar or cage, you may want to put a stone or other marker nearby to help you to recall the seed's location and to remind you to weed around it and to water it.

For the lucky ones among us with mature trees, seeds give us an easy way to share our garden's bounty with a family member, a friend, or a neighbor. Watching a native tree grow from seed is a priceless pleasure.

Start Cool-Season Grasses

Grasses are versatile elements in garden design. Planted symmetrically or on a grid, they punctuate a garden with architectural drama. As lawns, they provide a place for play and social gatherings. In drifts and meadows, they evoke nature. They are equally versatile in their acceptance of propagation and tending. They can be planted from gallon containers or plugs. They can be sown from seed or laid as sod. They can be left to grow on their own, cut back periodically, or mowed regularly. Many of California's native grasses, including needlegrass (*Achnatherum* spp.) and most fescues (*Festuca* spp.), are cool-season grasses. Now is the best time to get them established in the garden.

October is a particularly good time to create a meadow or lawn from seed sown directly in the ground. The heat waves are behind us, yet most of the state still has enough warmth for the seeds to germinate easily, and the days are still long enough to support their growth afterward. For lawns, rhizomous grasses—that is, those that send out horizontal underground shoots—should be used. The rhizomes help fill out the lawn. One of these rhizomous grasses is Diego bentgrass (*Agrostis pallens*). With mowing, it forms a thick, drought-tolerant turf that stays green all summer if watered every three weeks or so. With somewhat more moisture and infrequent mowing, red fescue (*Festuca rubra*) forms a fine, hummocky lawn that is soft and inviting. Indeed, some of the prettiest native "lawns" are those that are mowed only a few times a year. In most of the state, a lawn or meadow seeded in early October should be green by Thanksgiving.

If a lawn is wanted right away, native sod—usually bentgrass or a blend of fescues—can be laid. While many gardeners reckon that seed-sown grasses—native or not—ultimately establish themselves better than sod, there is no denying that sod provides a speedy result. Whether one is hurrying to prepare the lawn for a social event or simply wants to privately enjoy the garden right away, a native sod provides a good alternative to a nonnative one. Some of the commercially available sods should be mowed regularly, while others use grasses that can be mowed occasionally or left long and undulating. To conserve on the expense of sod, one might lay just a small patch where immediacy is most desired and seed a larger area around it at the same time. The surrounding seed might be the same mix of species that is present in the sod, or it might be interplanted with bulbs, wildflowers, and other grasses to provide a meadow in the background.

Regardless of whether you lay sod, sow for turf, or sow for a meadow, you should rid the soil of weeds ahead of time. Just as with annual wildflowers, you can water ahead to induce weeds to germinate, then hoe them over once they have come up. A hula hoe (also called a stirrup, action, swivel, or scuffle hoe) works very well for this. To establish a satisfactory lawn or meadow, weed germination and hoeing should be repeated at least one more time before sowing. If there is heavy germination in the second round, then follow up with a third round. Preparatory weeding should not be skipped, even for sod. Sod will smother some weeds, but aggressive ones (sourgrass, *oxalis pes-caprae*, for example) will come up right through it. So while sod provides an instant effect, the effect will not last if the ground has not been properly prepared ahead of time. Weed hard ahead; hardly weed later.

To plant this hummocky red fescue lawn, the author first cleared weeds, then used row cover after seeding. HELEN POPPER

Clean Up: Prune, Mulch, and Weed

Look around the garden for remaining deadwood, legginess, or spent flowers. Remove dead limbs from shrubs and trees now, before the Santa Anas or northern storm winds cause damage. Cut back mallow (*Malacothamnus* spp.) by a third or so; selectively thin redbud (*Cercis occidentalis*) and currant (*Ribes* spp.) to remove weak or crossing branches. If an old redbud is spent, you can coppice it (cut it to the ground) now, though it will take a long time to recover.

Rejuvenate perennials, such as asters, gumplants, monkeyflowers, and penstemons (*Aster, Grindelia, Mimulus,* and *Penstemon* spp.) by cutting them back now if you haven't yet, and if they are through blooming. You can also cut back buckwheats (*Eriogonum* spp.) if you like, but many gardeners prefer to leave their decorative seed heads on the plant for a while longer. Some perennials, such as sagebrush (*Artemisia* spp.) and island snapdragon (*Galvezia speciosa*), benefit from being cut back hard to prevent a woody buildup. For other perennials, use their new growth as a guide. If old woody stems have new growth, then you usually can cut back to that new growth. If they do not have new growth, then you can selectively remove a few branches, or you can try to promote side branching by pinching off just a bit at the very tips of the branches. If currants (*Ribes* spp.), some sages (such as creeping sage, *Salvia sonomensis*), and island snapdragons are producing new growth, then your pruning work will do double duty by providing cuttings as well as healthier parent plants.

Remove any mulch that may have built up around trunks or root crowns. Top off mulch where it is needed. When the rain arrives, it can bring a fresh crop of weeds, and mulch is helpful in keeping them at bay. However, you should not mulch where you plan to sow wildflowers or install native grasses from plugs, seed, or sod. Just as mulch keeps down young weeds, it also keeps down wildflowers and native grass seedlings. Hand-weed or hoe the areas you have newly cleared for wildflowers or grasses.

Water

Fall growth begins with rain, which may come early, late, or not at all this month. If the weather is drier than you had hoped, you can nudge fall growth forward with supplemental water as soon as the days begin to cool. You can also keep many flowers, such as sunflowers (*Helianthus annuus*), blooming longer with a little supplemental water.

Once you have sown or planted, you must water during any dry spells. Containers that await planting also need regular water. Consider the wind as well in your watering regimen. Wind dries out new plants quickly, so when you hear a forecast of dry winds, give your plants a drink. In the areas hit by the hot, dry Santa Anas, even established plants benefit from deep soaking ahead of the winds.

WHAT'S IN BLOOM?

While school bells sound in the distance and pumpkins bedeck front porches, clever gardeners enjoy a concoction of color blended from three seasons. The bold flowers of late summer combine with an echo of spring and the heralds of fall.

Having been deadheaded, monkeyflowers and yarrow rebloom in combination with fall's more traditional California asters. HELEN POPPER

Aspens give fall color to mountain gardens. JUDY KRAMER

A hot summer palette of red, yellow, and gold blazes through October. California fuchsias (*Epilobium* spp.) put out the hummingbird welcome sign of abundant orange-red, tubular flowers. The yellow members of the sunflower family, Asteraceae, parade on: annual sunflowers (*Helianthus annuus*) line the backs of borders; gumplants (*Grindelia stricta* var. *platyphylla*) spill sunny blooms over the edges of rock walls; and sweeps of California goldenrod (*Solidago californica*) support monarch butterflies in their fall migration.

A smattering of blue, lavender, lilac, and pink blooms also bridges summer and fall. With good drainage and just a bit of water, woolly blue curls (*Trichostema lanatum*) and lilac verbena (*Verbena lilacina*) continue to bloom. Pacific aster (*Aster chilensis*) and silver carpet California aster (*Lessingia filaginifolia* 'Silver Carpet') lend lavender and more lilac. Masses of ashy-leaf buckwheat (*Eriogonum cinereum*) add clouds of soft pink to the garden.

A subtle reprise of spring joins in. Renewed blooms open here and there on coyote mint, ceanothus, sage, and monkeyflower (*Monardella villosa,* and *Ceanothus, Salvia,* and *Mimulus* spp.). Late-sown wildflowers, such as ruby-chalice and punch-bowl godetia (*Clarkia rubicunda* and *C. bottae*), flower along with the occasional California poppy (*Eschscholzia californica*).

The lingering summer pleasures and little spring surprises might distract us from the first indications of fall, but the signs soon overwhelm us. They begin with the bright golds and yellows of big-leaf maples (*Acer macrophyllum*) in the north, California black walnuts (southern California's variety, *Juglans californica* var. *californica*) in the south, and quaking aspens (*Populus tremuloides*) and black oaks (*Quercus kelloggii*) in mountain gardens. Vine maples (*Acer circinatum*) turn red in the sun, and western redbuds (*Cercis occidentalis*) and California wild grapes (*Vitis californica*) follow. When the berries of the toyons (*Heteromeles arbutifolia*) begin to turn color, the trick-or-treaters come knocking, and so does fall.

Spring Is Here

November

In the great Central Valley of California there are only two seasons—spring and summer. The spring begins with the first rainstorm, which usually falls in November.—JOHN MUIR, *My First Summer in the Sierra,* 1911

The days are shorter, the air has cooled, and the first "spring" rains have soaked the soil. Tiny new wildflower seedlings coat once-bare earth with green fuzz, and grassy hillsides come alive. The leaves of sumac (*Rhus trilobata,* an innocent cousin of poison oak, *Toxicodendron diversilobum*) turn gold, red, and burgundy.

In the garden, the fall planting time has arrived in earnest. Now is the ideal time to plant bulbs and their kin and to plant oaks from acorns. In areas without serious freezes or major deer-grazing problems, it also is time to move nursery-grown plants from their containers into the ground and to sow the seeds of wildflowers. Whatever you plant this

❮ Oaks can be planted now. STEPHEN INGRAM

NOVEMBER'S JOBS

A QUICK LOOK

Plant bulbs and their brethren

Bulbs store nutrients until the right time arrives to send up shoots. Plant them now. They will emerge soon with an early promise of spring.

Plant oaks

Acorns germinate well now, and seedlings get a good start. Water them in well, and protect them from predation.

Sow seeds

Weed thoroughly, then sow seeds. Sow wildflowers in waves for a long spring show. Sow easy-germinating perennials too, and try your hand at direct-sowing a few shrubs.

Plant from containers

In mild-winter areas, continue to plant from containers. Plant when the soil is moist but not sodden.

Divide plants

Divide cool-season grasses, along with irises (*Iris* spp.), coral bells (*Heuchera* spp.), and other perennials that will bloom in spring.

Take cuttings

Take hardwood cuttings from young growth on shrubs and stem cuttings from sages (*Salvia* spp.).

Practice good grooming

Sages will set their buds soon for their spring bloom. Prune them now so you won't miss out on the flowers. Cut back large, established perennials, such as Matilija poppy (*Romneya coulteri*). Pinch shrubs to keep them filled out. Weed around seedlings and small plants. Mulch around shrubs and trees.

month, situate the plants according to their needs, and prepare the site by eliminating weeds.

NATIVE GARDENING IN NOVEMBER
Plant Bulbs and Their Brethren

Bulbs, corms, tubers, and rhizomes store life underground for a quiet time, often a period of complete dormancy. When the rains come, life begins anew. By winter, we see green shoots, then leaves. In spring, if enough energy has been stored below, their drama unfolds above. Leopard lilies (*Lilium pardalinum*) startle us with a cascade of bold spotted blooms on head-high stalks. The delicate white blooms of fairy lanterns (*Calochortus albus*) seem to glow at our feet. Quivers of Ithuriel's spears (*Triteleia laxa*) punctuate a meadow. The flowers captivate us, but as gardeners, we must attend to their underground lives.

Many bulbs and their brethren are fastidious about water in their dormant period. Most of California's bulbs require drought during their quiet phase, and a combination of water and heat will kill them. Others simply need good drainage. Still others—generally those from the state's cool-summer areas—require year-round moisture. Situate bulbs now where you will be able to meet their requirements in summer.

If you have your heart set on bulbs that do not quite fit your garden's conditions, you can grow them in a pot or other container. You can move a pot around to suit the bulbs and to suit yourself, enjoying the flowers when they look their best. Just remember, planting natives in containers is a little different from planting them in the ground. When you plant in containers, the plants rely on you for everything, including nutrients. While fertilizer rarely helps natives when they are planted in the ground, mild fertilizer does help container-grown natives, including bulbs.

Like all plants, bulbs need some freedom from competition and predation. Once you decide where to plant them, clear the area of weeds. Competition also can come from non-weedy natives. Grasses, in particular, can impede bulb development. While many native bulbs do thrive in wild meadows, newly planted bulbs have a hard time competing with well-established grasses in a garden. Among mature grasses, they do better if they are planted from containers, which afford them some soil and surface to themselves.

To protect against rodents, tuck the bulbs into rock walls or use wire gopher baskets. The baskets protect the bulbs from below and from the sides. Slender-shooted bulbs that can find their way through the spaces in wire mesh can be safeguarded with mesh across the top as well. Cut the top mesh to about six inches across, bending down the edges if you like. Then bury it about an inch below the surface of the soil. A few bulbs, such as those of Ithuriel's spear (*Triteleia laxa*) and one-leaf onion (*Allium unifolium*), are popular throughout the country and indeed the world. These bulbs are easy to find and relatively inexpensive, so you may be willing to risk planting them without the work and expense of gopher baskets. Pungent alliums may not appeal much to gophers anyway. For more prized bulbs, the gopher baskets are worth the effort.

Some gardeners plant bulbs using a dibble, which is nothing more than a tapered stick used to poke the planting hole. Typically, the dibble is marked at various lengths, and it is used to plant many bulbs, one right after another, without baskets. Whether you dibble or use a trowel, the rule of thumb in planting bulbs is to allow at least an inch of space between them, and to plant them about three times deeper than their longest dimension.

The bulbs will not need to be watered again until they sprout. Once they do sprout, they will need periodic water, whether from rain or irrigation, until they bloom. You may want to mark the planting areas while you can still recall where the bulbs are. Some take more than a year to flower. Once established, though, bulbs will reward you with blooms year after year.

Plant Oaks

Oaks find their way into our hearts and our gardens. A scrub oak (*Quercus berberidifolia,* or possibly *Q. dumosa*) carves a pocket of wilderness out of an urban garden. With more space, coast live oaks (*Q. agrifolia*) sprawl out luxuriously to shade old suburban avenues. Valley oaks (*Q. lobata*), stately and tall, preside over rural dales. For these and other native oaks, planting in November's rain-soaked soils provides a nice long time for their roots to establish themselves before the rains cease in spring.

If you will be planting oaks where you are unlikely to irrigate, consider planting acorns. While many acorns will be lost to predators, the survivors will form roots that are well adapted to irregular watering. From direct-planted acorns, tap roots extend quickly down into the soil. They anchor the plant deep below and branch out to the side only later, after the green shoots emerge in December. In contrast, the tap roots of typical container plants are tip pruned (to prevent the root from circling), and the plants luxuriate in the nursery soil and branch profusely from the get-go. This root structure supports their growth above and makes transplanting them from containers easy. However, it is the upper portion of the soil that dries out first when the rains abate, so the shallow container-formed roots are less effective during dry spells than the deep acorn-planted roots. Acorns are a good choice now if water may not be abundant later in the year.

Although many acorns germinate best after being refrigerated for a month, the acorns of coast live oaks are a notable exception. These germinate after their first soaking, and they germinate well if they do not dry out, so plant them soon after you collect them. Some gardeners add small rocks to the planting hole and the area above to deter rodents. For greater protection, you can use a commercial tree shelter or install wire mesh cylinders that extend a foot or more above the soil and several inches below. Alternatively, you can bury a one-quart plastic tub (with the bottom removed) to make an underground collar around the acorn and beneath the wire mesh. Even with this protection, predators will find some of the acorns, and not all of those that are left will germinate. Plant extras.

Whether you plant from acorns or containers, start with well-moistened soil and clear weeds within a foot of the planting hole. Weeds compete with the oaks and provide cover for small browsers. If you are planting an acorn, dig the hole a few inches deep, then backfill and tamp down a bit to make the soil hospitable to new roots. Lay the acorn on its side (both roots and shoots come from the pointed end) and bury it under an inch of soil. If you plant your oak from a nursery container, treat it like other natives. Dig a hole roughly twice as wide and somewhat deeper than the container—deep enough to ensure that the roots can lie comfortably without coiling. Scuff the sides of the planting hole, and do not amend the soil. By scuffing, you make it easier for the roots to find their way into the surrounding soil; by omitting amendments, you encourage them to do so. Position the plant so that its crown ends up just slightly higher than the surface of the surrounding soil. As with acorns, backfill and tamp down the soil. Like acorns, newly planted saplings can suffer from predation, so you may want to surround the young plants with the same kind of wire cylinders used for acorns, or with commercial tree shelters.

Water the newly planted acorns or young plants well. Then mulch around the area (but not directly over the acorn or the plant's stem) to retain moisture and keep weeds at bay. Water again during any prolonged winter dry spells. If you have installed protective shelters, check on the plants from time to time to see if their growth is overtaking the shelters, which you will then need to enlarge or remove, and take out any vigorous weeds. Water occasionally, but deeply, through the remainder of at least the first year, and perhaps the second. After that, a well-situated oak can get by on rainfall alone as long as there are not too many weeds. While some oaks—particularly blue oaks (*Quercus douglasii*)—have a reputation for growing slowly, forestry research suggests the reputation is largely undeserved. With enough water and protection from browsing, even a blue oak will stand more than head high by its fourth year, and its growth will then begin to accelerate. The beautiful tree you once saw only in your imagination will start to take shape before you.

Sow Seeds

November is a wonderful time to sow seeds in all but the coldest areas of California. Wildflowers germinate readily with the month's rains, and their seeds can be sown in waves over time to keep blooms coming month after month. While most perennial seeds are best sown in flats, some free-flowering ones can be sown in the ground now. Even the seeds of some woody perennials can be directly sown, under the right garden conditions.

Sown now, annual wildflower seeds demand very little from us. "A very good time is just before a rain, or even while it is raining, if it can be so arranged," observed the famed horticulturalist Theodore Payne in 1910. Winter rains are likely to give wildflowers most or all of the water they need. As gardeners, our role is to select the right flowers for our garden conditions and get them off to a good start by eradicating weeds before sowing seeds. Once most weeds have been removed, as described in the previous chapter, we can sow wildflower seeds every few weeks, now and through the rest of fall and winter. With occasional weeding and watering, the repeated sowing will deliver a procession of color.

While annual seeds germinate readily, perennials are trickier. In nature, many seeds fail. Some wait years to germinate, sometimes doing so only after having been charred by fire. Others lose their viability before a year is out and germinate only in response to being digested by animals or left in the cold. In a garden setting, some perennial seeds require artificial pretreatment (with hydrogen peroxide, boiling water, or even smoke) followed by careful tending in flats. Others, however, can be sown directly.

Among perennials, the best candidates for direct sowing are the herbaceous ones that readily self-sow. Blue flax (*Linum lewisii*), for example, whose delicate morning blooms return year after year, is notorious for spreading throughout the garden. Its seeds need no pretreatment. Other well-known self-sowers include pearly everlasting (*Anaphalis margaritacea*), woolly sunflower (*Eriophyllum lanatum*), and yarrow (*Achillea millefolium*), all of which bloom robustly and make good cut flowers. The

Blue flax readily self-sows.
HELEN POPPER

seeds of these herbaceous perennials germinate easily and can be sown like those of annuals.

The seeds of many woody perennials also can be directly sown now, but they should be sown more like acorns. Gardeners have had success with fall sowing of coyote bush (*Baccharis pilularis*), giant buckwheat (*Eriogonum arborescens*), and purple sage (*Salvia leucophylla*) on the dry slopes of coastal scrub and chaparral gardens, and western spicebush (*Calycanthus occidentalis*) along creeks and near ponds.

For woody perennials, dig a hole a few inches deep and break up the soil if it is compacted. Then backfill it a bit. Plant one or two or up to a dozen seeds in the hole, depending on their size and expected germination. Germination rates vary, but germination tends to be better in species with large seeds than species with small seeds, particularly in unfavorable weather. Tiny seedlings are easily lost to predation, so if you have the time, protect them with the same kind of wire cylinders or collars used for acorns. Plant the seeds two or three times as deep as their diameter, and very gently tamp down the soil. Later, you can cull any extra seedlings that might come up. If the extras are packed in tight, pulling them out might tear the roots of the one you plan to keep, so cut the extras back with scissors instead. Water the seeds in well, and mulch around, not over, where you have sown. Keep the area weeded, and if the rains are sparse give seedlings some extra water to help get them established.

Berry producers, such as holly-leaf cherry (*Prunus ilicifolia*) and coffee-berry (*Rhamnus californica*), often come up best when their berries are fresh and the seeds have been separated from the pulp. One way to separate the pulp is simply to let the berries rot in water for a week. Coffeeberry seeds will germinate even if they are picked slightly unripe—a week or two early—but the berries of the toyon (*Heteromeles arbutifolia*) need to be quite ripe. They color up before they are completely ripe, so wait until the end of the month, then confirm that the seeds inside are firm before picking the berries. In some areas, toyon berries won't ripen until December. In the wild, many of the berry-producing shrubs come up consistently only during wet years. This gives us a cue for the garden: provide ample water if the rains do not.

Plant from Containers

In much of the state, November is the best time to plant from containers. November's rains have softened the soil, and their increasing reliability eases the task of follow-up watering. Sustained rains can have a drawback, however. In some years, pounding rains can leave the soil—especially heavy clay soil—too sodden for garden work. If the soil adheres to your shovel blade, glomming onto it even when you turn the blade over, then give the soil and yourself a rest. Try again in a day or two. Ideally, the soil will fall freely when you turn over your shovel blade, and it will break apart when it hits the ground.

When the soil is moist but not sodden, it is easy to clear weeds and dig the planting hole. Moving aside any mulch, dig the hole about twice as wide and just a bit deeper than the container. Scuff up the sides of the hole so the roots can make their way beyond it. Break up any large clods and backfill the hole just enough to mound up the soil slightly in the center. The mound will make it easier for you to stretch out any roots that you uncoil, and it will help you keep the ultimate height of the plant's crown above the surrounding soil level. Gently ease the plant out of its container. Free up coiled, tangled, or turned-back roots, and position the plant on the mound with any dangling roots nicely spread around it. Backfill the hole, water the plant in well, and mulch around it. Be prepared with follow-up water when the rains abate.

Divide Plants

Once established in our gardens, some plants cry out for division. Irises (*Iris* spp.) spread over time, and their beauty compels us to find more homes for them in our garden and with our friends. Division lets us share them with ease. Coral bells (*Heuchera* spp.), lovely as they are, lose vigor as they age, as do many native grasses. Division rejuvenates them. Woodland strawberries (*Fragaria vesca*) offer up natural divisions on runners: offsets that are already separated from the parent plants. "Dividing" them requires nothing more than leaving them in place or lifting them to plant in a new location. For these and many other spring-blooming natives, now is a good time for division.

When the plants are ready to be divided, water them well, and water their ultimate location too. Irises are ready for division when little pink or white roots appear at the edge of the fan of leaves. The new growth indicates that the roots are active and are likely to survive division. Even so, experienced gardeners don't divide all their irises in one year. For irises and many other plants, division risks more losses than planting from containers. Moisture is key. With container planting, the roots stay safely ensconced in a root ball, where soil protects them from the drying air.

With division, one severs the soil-root connection. Exposed to the air, roots can desiccate with prolonged handling and delayed relocation. So choose a cool, calm day for division and be prepared to replant right away.

Once everything is ready, loosen the soil around the plant with your shovel. Then gently lift the plant with its roots attached. Inspect both the roots and the leaves to see where the plant seems to divide naturally to form individual smaller plants. Each "plantlet" should be complete with roots and shoots. Pull apart or cleanly cut the plant at those natural divisions.

You now have several plants where you previously had just one. Take a look at each. Moisture is taken in through roots and lost through leaves, so the roots need to be large enough to balance the leafy surface area. If any of the newly wrought individuals seems very top heavy, judiciously cut away one or a few of its leaves. Then plant the divisions as you would any other new plant, but give them extra water until their roots have had a chance to grow. For irises, be especially careful to plant them with their crowns somewhat higher than the surrounding soil.

In addition to irises, grasses, and coral bells, many other natives can be divided now, including blue-eyed grass (*Sisyrinchium bellum*), butterfly weed (*Asclepias tuberosa*), hummingbird sage (*Salvia spathacea*), Matilija poppy (*Romneya coulteri*), and slim Solomon's seal (*Smilacina stellata*). Among the easiest are California fuchsia (*Epilobium* spp.), Pacific bleeding heart (*Dicentra formosa*), and wild ginger (*Asarum caudatum*). California fuchsia can be divided successfully from roots even when the foliage has died back completely. Bleeding heart and wild ginger, along with coral bells, form wide mats with roots throughout, so dividing them is uncomplicated. Coral bells show you they are ready for division when the base becomes stalk-like. Bury this after division. For all of these mat-forming perennials, simply slip a sharp spade into the plant and lift off sections that have both foliage and roots. These are your new "plantlets."

A full clump of fairybells is divided into smaller plants.
PAUL FURMAN

Take Cuttings

Walk out in the morning, when plants hold the most moisture, and take cuttings. This month, take softwood cuttings from the branch tips of kinnikinnick (*Arctostaphylos uva-ursi*) and of sages (*Salvia* spp.) as you prune them. Take hardwood cuttings from coffeeberry (*Rhamnus californica*), California huckleberry (*Vaccinium ovatum*), common snowberry (*Symphoricarpos albus*), and twinberry (*Lonicera involucrata*). Most gardeners recommend taking cuttings that are a quarter to a half inch thick, although others suggest that cuttings should be about an eighth of an inch, less than pencil thickness. Include four to six nodes, which will usually be spread along a four- or five-inch length. Twinberry may have nodes that are farther apart, so its cuttings might be longer, up to ten inches. Longer cuttings also can work, as can "stakes," even longer, thicker cuttings that are planted directly into the ground. Huckleberry may be the most difficult to root. To improve your huckleberry prospects, use new, unbranched growth and take three sets of cuttings three weeks apart. Only one is likely to take. For any cutting, choose a healthy stem and angle the bottom cut to remind you which side goes down into the soil or rooting medium. Keep the cuttings cool and moist as you continue your collecting.

To prepare each cutting, remove all the leaves or buds from its bottom half. Water is lost through leaves, and new cuttings have no roots yet to compensate. If the top half is leafy, remove or cut some of the upper leaves as well. For most cuttings, it's helpful to treat the lower, diagonal end of the cutting with rooting hormone before placing it into moist soil or rooting medium. Added now, rooting hormone improves the speed and consistency of rooting for most plants. A few gardeners also recommend inoculating the potting medium (coarse sand, or a mixture of coarse sand and vermiculite, perlite, or peat) with a spoonful of the parent plant's soil to establish the parent's beneficial fungi.

Strike the angled bottom end of the cuttings about two to two and a half inches into the medium. For soft cuttings, you may want to poke a hole into the medium with a pencil first. Mist the plants often to keep them moist until they root.

Resist the urge to jiggle the plants or examine their roots. (If you can't stop yourself, give over a single sacrificial cutting to your curiosity.) Wait for the first sign of new growth above the rooting medium before you disturb them. You are likely to see new growth after a month or two. When you do, it is time to transplant the cuttings into a small pot with soil. As mentioned earlier, plants in pots rely on you for all their needs, so you may want to add fertilizer. With the exception of the hard-to-root huckleberry, expect about half to three-quarters of your cuttings to survive. By next fall, you can plant them in the garden or share them with friends.

Practice Good Grooming

Tidy up this month by mulching, weeding, and pruning. If your garden has deciduous trees, then you have a fresh source of organic mulch: fallen leaves. Pull the leaf litter—along with other mulch—away from root crowns, and clear it off newly seeded areas and low-growing plants that it might smother. As for the rest of the leaf litter, leave it in place. In contact with the soil, the leaves will break down over winter into leaf mold, improving the soil's structure and adding nutrients. Like other mulch, leaf litter will protect the soil from erosion and you from mud, provide a lovely carpet under shrubs and trees, and help shrink this month's weeding job.

Pruning may take a little extra time this month. Many native perennials benefit from regular, sometimes dramatic, pruning in late fall. Matilija poppy (*Romneya coulteri*) rejuvenates itself beautifully after being cut back to about six inches or so, either now or in December. Seaside daisy (*Erigeron glaucus*) and goldenaster (*Heterotheca sessiliflora*) can be cut back to

A fall trimming gives seaside daisy a nice spring shape. JUDY KRAMER

37

two inches. Canyon Prince wild rye (*Leymus condensatus* 'Canyon Prince') can be cut to the ground every few years, and canyon sunflower (*Venegasia carpesioides*) and climbing penstemon (*Keckiella cordifolia*) can be cut back by half. Vigorous sages, such as Cleveland sage (*Salvia clevelandii*), can be cut back by a third, though not to old wood. Sage should be cut back now before the buds set, so you can enjoy blooms in spring. Every few years—whenever it starts to look shabby—California fuchsia (*Epilobium* spp.) should be cut back nearly to the ground. Light pruning helps many other perennials maintain a fresh form. Lightly trimming new growth of bush monkeyflower (*Mimulus* spp.), sagebrush (*Artemisia* spp.), and coyote mint (*Monardella villosa*) keeps them from getting leggy.

Some shrubs, too, benefit from pruning. Sugar bush (*Rhus ovata*) will fill out with pinching. If redwood (*Sequoia sempervirens*) is kept as a hedge, this is the time to shear it. Removing the top third of mallow (*Malacothamnus* spp.)—or even coppicing it after some years—seems to increase its longevity. Mountain mahogany (*Cercocarpus betuloides*) can be pruned now to keep it narrow or to shape it as a small tree. Jojoba (*Simmondsia chinensis*) can be sheared to keep it as a hedge. Both mountain mahogany and jojoba can be coppiced now, if needed. (For more on coppicing, see the discussion in March, page 91.) Toyon (*Heteromeles arbutifolia*) can be pruned now if necessary, but it can wait. Its berries are beautiful on the shrub. Enjoy them in the garden for a while.

WHAT'S IN BLOOM?

The rugged beauty of a chaparral garden softens in fall. Bronze masses of California buckwheat (*Eriogonum fasciculatum*) billow along the edge of a path. Up the slope behind them, the gray-white bark of a buckeye (*Aesculus californica*) stands in silhouette against a blue storm-cleared sky. A few of its still-dangling seeds whimsically foreshadow Christmas ornaments. Woolly blue curls (*Trichostema lanatum*) bloom at the end of scented stems nearby, and the puffy seed heads of pipestem clematis (also known as chaparral clematis, *Clematis lasiantha*) spill out over the top of a fence.

In a coastal cottage garden, the cheerful lavender flowers of Pacific aster (*Aster chilensis*) combine prettily with the bright yellow tarweed (*Madia*

elegans) still blooming behind them. Bush sunflower (*Encelia californica*) vies for our attention. All are backed by a loose semicircle of evergreen shrubs—island bush poppy (*Dendromecon harfordii*), which is brightened by still more yellow flowers.

November brings fewer flowers but more traditional fall color to a moist woodland garden. The leaves of vine maple (*Acer circinatum*) have turned a fiery red. In a shady border, the little yellow flowers of redwood violet (*Viola sempervirens*) punctuate their own green carpet. Behind them, the white globes of snowberry (*Symphoricarpos albus*) gleam on otherwise bare stems. In the background, the low autumn sun catches the leaves of a western spicebush (*Calycanthus occidentalis*)—some still bright green, others now lemon yellow. The combination of colors—especially the red vine maple, yellow spicebush, and white snowberry—invites us to decorate a centerpiece just in time for Thanksgiving dinner.

❰ Buckwheats carry their tawny hues for months. KEITH PHILLIPS

❱ Vine maple colors up in fall. SAXON HOLT

December

In the late morning after a storm, oak branches emerge out of the mist like ghosts. Raindrops cling to the serrated margins of toyon leaves. Maple leaves rest on the garden floor. All is moist, cool, and quiet.

Bare branches reveal the structure of once-leafy shrubs. Guided by their undisguised contours, we can judiciously prune them while they are dormant. We then can take our clippers and loppers to the herbaceous perennials that have soldiered on through fall. Once they are cleaned up, we can amble around the garden with a basket to collect the right evergreens, berries, pinecones, and more to bring inside or hang on the door in a spray or a wreath.

Those of us who have sown wildflower seeds or let the past year's bounty go to seed will begin to anticipate our reward now. As the day brightens, fresh green seedlings

◀ Coffeeberry provides winter color. SAXON HOLT

DECEMBER'S JOBS

Sow seeds

The berries of toyons *(Heteromeles arbutifolia)* ripen this month. Soak the berries to remove their pulp before sowing the seeds. Sow acorns, iris seeds, and annual wildflower seeds too.

Divide

Many actively growing perennials can be divided now, including cool-season grasses, sedges, rushes, and irises. Stream orchids (*Epipactis gigantea*) are best divided when they are dormant, usually near the end of the month.

Plant and transplant

In mild-winter areas, you can plant from nursery containers now, and you can transplant any volunteers that have popped up in the wrong place.

Propagate with cuttings

Take cuttings from branching dudleyas. Take hardwood cuttings from berry-bearing plants, such as currants (*Ribes* spp.), after they lose their leaves.

Prune

Cut back herbaceous perennials and pinch shrubs that are still blooming. Clean up coyote bushes (*Baccharis pilularis*) and roses (*Rosa* spp.) if they have become patchy. Prune toyons (*Heteromeles arbutifolia*) and deciduous trees if they need it.

Control ants and gophers

Argentine ants are bad enough in the garden, where they harbor aphids and other honeydew-producing insects. In winter, they sometimes move indoors in search of food. Gophers become most active when the soil is moist, and they can destroy bulbs and perennials as fast as we can plant them. Protect your favorite plants with gopher wire.

Tidy up and follow up

Weed, mulch, make repairs, and water your new plantings if rains are absent.

Bring garden trimmings inside

Use conifers, California bay laurel (*Umbellularia californica*), wax myrtle (*Myrica californica*), and toyon (*Heteromeles arbutifolia*) to make traditional wreaths, sprays, and garlands. Or reinterpret ancient winter traditions with other long-lasting foliage from the garden, such as live oak (*Quercus* spp.), manzanita (*Arctostaphylos* spp.), coffeeberry (*Rhamnus californica*), and Oregon grape (*Berberis* spp.).

buoy us with their promise of spring. We can help them along by weeding around them. The seedlings in our own garden or elsewhere remind us that still more seeds can be sown in December.

NATIVE GARDENING IN DECEMBER
Sow Seeds: Toyon and More

This is the season for toyon (*Heteromeles arbutifolia*). Equally at home in formal and informal settings, toyon blends into the garden and provides a serene green backdrop throughout the year. Now its bright red berries capture our attention and announce the holidays. Toyon is sometimes aptly called Christmas berry or California holly, and its copious berries feed cedar waxwings and scores of other birds. The large shrubs grace the open chaparral and woodlands from Oregon to Mexico. We can enjoy them and the birds they attract in our own gardens, where we also can collect their berry clusters for decoration and for seed.

To sow toyon seeds, harvest the berries late in the month when they are fully ripe, and cover them with water. Let them soak for a week. The fleshy fruit will soften and pull away easily from the seeds. To dislodge the seed from what is left of the fruit, squish each berry or use a rolling pin over the lot of them. Then gently wash away the flesh and skin with more water. It is best to sow the fresh seeds right away, either into small pots or directly into the soil. Follow up with moisture, and perhaps with shade and leaf litter to nurture the young seedlings when they come up. If you wait a while before sowing the seeds, they will go dormant. Once dormant, the seeds must be left in the refrigerator for three months before they can be sown. So sow them now, when they are fresh: it's the right time and the easy time.

Many other seeds also can be sown now, including those of iris (*Iris* spp.), buckeye (*Aesculus californica*), oak (*Quercus* spp.), and most wildflowers. Iris seeds will take a few months to germinate, and some of the seeds won't germinate until the following year. Sow them where they won't be bothered, either under shrubs or other perennials or in pots. Buckeye seeds will germinate almost anywhere with moisture. Acorns can be sown directly too, as described on page 29. Continue to sow annual wildflowers

Twinberry seeds can be separated from the pulp by mashing the berries. JACKIE PASCOE

to encourage a long spring show. While a few of them are robust enough to out-compete many weeds, most are not, so weed first, then seed. Or sow them in weed-free pots and enjoy their spring show wherever you like.

Divide

This month, we can still divide cool-season grasses, sedges, rushes, irises, and *Sisyrinchium*, such as blue-eyed and yellow-eyed grass (*S. bellum* and *S. californicum*). We also can divide self-heal (*Prunella vulgaris*) and piggy-back plant (*Tolmiea menziesii,* often sold as a house plant). (For more on dividing plants, see the discussion in November, pages 33–35.)

Late in the month, we can divide stream orchids (*Epipactis gigantea*). While we divide irises and many other plants when they show new signs of growth, we wait to divide stream orchids until they have clearly entered their winter dormancy. They usually die back to the ground and are ready for division near the end of the month. Start by preparing a moist location for the new divisions, perhaps near a creek or in a large tub. Then return to the stream orchids and loosen the soil around them. Carefully lift the (rather thin) rhizomes with their long roots attached. In each clump of rhizomes, look at the location of its growth buds. Making sure each divided piece will have several buds, cut the rhizomes with a sharp knife. Gently untangle the roots to separate them. Replant them right away in their new location.

Plant and Transplant

In most of the state, the winters are mild enough that we can keep planting from containers right through the cool months. Winter rains soften the soil, making it easy to work. However, after an especially long, hard rain, let the sodden soil dry out a bit before planting. If your planting is followed by a dry spell, give supplemental water until the rains return. It takes time for plants to establish roots.

As our gardens mature, seedlings of established shrubs and trees begin to volunteer, sometimes in surprising places. When they sprout up in just the right spot, we can let them grow. Sometimes, though, we can't leave them where they are. Whether the volunteers are currants (*Ribes* spp.), holly-leaf cherries (*Prunus ilicifolia*), dormant vine maple seedlings (*Acer circinatum*), or something else that thrives in your garden, this is a good time to transplant the ones that must move.

Go out when the ground is moist and thrust your spade into the soil of the plant's new, more appropriate home. Just wiggle the spade a bit to create a gap in the soil—do not bother to dig up even a single shovelful of dirt. A crevice is enough. Then go back to your little volunteer and use your spade to lift it out, along with some soil to protect the roots. You might be tempted to use a trowel, but be prepared for roots that are long relative to the little seedling. Volunteers can surprise us with roots that are longer than their nursery-grown counterparts. Gently plant the volunteer, along with the soil around the roots, in the new crevice. Close the gap back up, and mulch around the volunteer in its new home. Keep it watered as you would to establish any other new young plant.

Propagate with Cuttings

December is a good time to take hardwood cuttings. Gardeners have had success with cuttings from the mature stems of flowering shrubs, such as wild mock orange (*Philadelphus lewisii*) and Douglas' spirea (*Spiraea douglasii*). Spirea is especially easy: you can skip the pots and plant the cuttings in the garden the same day. Berry-bearing shrubs, such as California blackberry and salmonberry (*Rubus ursinus* and *R. spectabilis*) and pink-flowering and golden currants (*Ribes sanguineum* and *R. aureum*), are also good candidates for December cuttings. Take cuttings (again) from California huckleberry (*Vaccinium ovatum*). It is hard to time the huckleberries just right, so take cuttings of them every three weeks or so, and expect only one set of cuttings to succeed. Prepare your cuttings as described on pages 35–37. With rooting hormone, successful cuttings from most of these plants will be ready to pot up in about six to eight weeks.

This is also a good time to take cuttings of branching dudleyas (*Dudleya* spp.). Plumped up after the rains, they begin their growing season now. Usually the main challenge of propagating with cuttings is keeping them moist. Propagating dudleyas from cuttings is a little different. For branching dudleyas, take a cutting of a side piece and set it aside for a couple of days to dry. Then rooting is easy, with or without hormones.

Prune

This is the time to prune many herbaceous perennials that have hung on through fall. Deadhead quail bush (*Atriplex lentiformis*) and big sagebrush (*Artemisia tridentata*), and cut California sagebrush (*A. californica*) back by half. Some perennials rejuvenate themselves most beautifully after being cut back quite hard. Among these are canyon sunflower (*Venegasia carpesioides*) and bush sunflower (*Encelia californica*), which—once established—can be cut back to under a foot. Both California fuchsia (*Epilobium* spp.) and mugwort (*Artemisia douglasiana*) will come back much prettier if they are mown nearly to the ground after a couple of years. Pinch back shrubs that continue to bloom, such as island bush poppy (*Dendromecon harfordii*).

Some plants benefit from being cut back hard only from time to time. Common tule (*Schoenoplectus acutus*) and Leopold's rush (*Juncus acutus* ssp. *leopoldii*) grow at the edges of ponds and marshes. They are large and usually quite beautiful, but they can get untidy after some years. They will grow back cleanly after being cut back. Pruning Leopold's rush takes some care, since its leaves are sharp. Established stands of coyote bush (*Baccharis pilularis*) and native rose (*Rosa californica* and *R. gymnocarpa*) can get patchy. If so, they may be pruned substantially or even coppiced.

A cedar waxwing enjoys a bounty of toyon berries. JAY THESKEN

Toyon (*Heteromeles arbutifolia*) could have been pruned modestly earlier, but waiting until mid- or late December is more satisfying. It allows the berries to ripen—for birds, for our own enjoyment on the shrub, for use in decorations, and for seed. With enough space, a toyon will grow into a beautiful, full shrub. Pinching it back a little each year will keep it dense. Toyon also can be trained into a small multi-trunked tree. For a tree, forgo the pinching and instead selectively remove some lower branches over the years. As you prune, keep in mind that its flowers will set on new growth in early spring. Pruning now—before the buds set—will yield the most flowers and berries next fall.

By now, many deciduous plants have lost most of their leaves. A plant's new leaflessness tells us it is dormant and ready for any pruning that might be needed. Its bareness also reveals the plant's structure, which should guide our pruning decisions. Trees, such as California black walnut (*Juglans californica*), Fremont cottonwood (*Populus fremontii*), elderberry (*Sambucus* spp.), and deciduous oak (*Quercus* spp.), may be pruned when they lose their leaves, if needed. So, too, may shrubs such as creek dogwood (*Cornus sericea,* which provides beautiful red stems for bouquets) and western spicebush (*Calycanthus occidentalis*).

Control Ants and Gophers

ARGENTINE ANTS Argentine ants are primarily garden pests that nurture aphids and other troublesome honeydew producers. However, they often invade homes when honeydew becomes scarce in winter. When ants do invade, wipe them away and clean the area with soapy water. The foraging ants leave a scent for others to follow, and the soapy water alone will remove the traces of it. Additional sprays are not needed. To keep new foraging troops out, seal off places where ants can enter the house, including cracks around plumbing or window sills. Next year's winter ant problems can be lessened by controlling the ant and aphid populations in spring. In the meantime, if soap and entry barriers are not enough to keep ants away, you can use bait stations along their trails. Compared with spraying and dusting, the stations allow less poison to reach children, pets, other animals, and the watershed. The bait stations house slow-acting poison that allows ants to live long enough to carry the poison back to the nest. Place the bait stations outside, where they will not entice ants into the house while you wait for the poison to work on the colony.

GOPHERS Gophers are most active in California when the soil is moist, so you may see gopher activity in your garden now, even if they left little trace all summer. In winter, a single gopher may make two or three mounds in a day. Gophers live mostly below ground, eating roots, but they occasionally eat above ground near their tunnel openings. It is near an opening that you might spot one. Or without seeing an animal at all, you may temporarily disbelieve your eyes as, in a matter of seconds, a perennial cartoonishly disappears into the ground.

Dealing with gophers is tricky. Excluding them is one option. You can protect specific plants, raised beds, or—if your garden is small—the entire property. For individual plants, you can use underground wire gopher baskets. Use generously sized baskets (say, a three-gallon basket for a one-gallon plant), so there will be ample room for the plant to grow. You can protect raised beds by stretching gopher wire across the bottom of them. To deter gophers from chewing up irrigation pipes, surround the pipes with gravel. For lawns and meadows, you can bury gopher wire a few inches below ground. To keep gophers out of an entire small garden, you can surround the whole garden with a miniature underground fence. Make it about two feet deep and turn a few additional inches outward, to deter gophers from digging deeper. Leave six inches above ground if you don't already have a solid fence. Gophers occasionally move above ground to gain access to new areas. This will deter most gophers from entering.

If you garden in an area that is good habitat for barn owls and your property is quite large, you might consider putting up a barn owl nest box. A barn owl won't rid your property of all gophers, but it will put a big dent in the local population. Barn owls are said to glide at least fifty or a hundred yards away from their nest before hunting, so do not put the nest box close to the problem area. When choosing a site for the nest box, you should also keep in mind that young barn owls are noisy at night.

Other options for gophers include traps, poisons, fast-flooding combined with shovel-killing, and learning to live with them. Living with gophers might mean protecting individual plants with wire baskets and otherwise excluding the gophers from small areas, while letting other garden areas have a more naturalistic look, where their hills will not be so out of place. The unprotected areas of the garden should rely less on perennials and extra water.

Gophers move around quite a bit in large expanses of tunnels. Judging whether or not a particular gopher management method (aside from a trap) works is tricky. An ineffective method might seem to work if the gopher disappears for a while in one of its episodic vacations to the neighbor's side of its maze. When the gopher later returns, the gardener may naturally think it is a new gopher. Such experiences make it easy to cling to the mistaken belief that a particular useless deterrent actually works. Look to field trials for evidence of effectiveness before wasting time on scare tactics, gopher purge, chewing gum, or expensive noisemakers and electronic devices. Don't be lured into using dangerous and ineffectual home remedies, such as strewing broken glass or worse.

❰ Laid a few inches deep, gopher wire protects part of the author's garden. HELEN POPPER

❧ A telltale mound builds up on one side of a gopher's hole. HELEN POPPER

Moles, which also tunnel underground, do not make a habit of eating roots or pulling down plants. Instead, they eat mainly grubs, earthworms, snails, and slugs. You are unlikely to see them, but you can tell them apart from gophers by their mounds. Gopher mounds look something like mine tailings: fan-shaped, with the soil plug at the narrow end. Mole hills usually are volcano shaped—they are round when viewed from above. If you can see the mole's soil plug, you'll find it in the center. Moles tunnel shallowly when the soil is moist, so you may see signs of their tunnels raised above soil level. They are generally beneficial in the garden. Unless you are bothered by their tunneling, you should leave them alone.

Tidy Up and Follow Up

Weed, mulch, make repairs, and water. Pull up or hoe nonnative grasses that pop up where they are not wanted. Use leaf litter as mulch: move it from where there is too much to where it is needed. Inspect your garden's hardscape. Retaining walls can give way with heavy, wet soil behind them; wind and rain can place a strain on fences, pergolas, and other garden structures. Repair them now to prevent further damage, both to the structures and to the plants around them. Finally, even in December we can find ourselves without rain. Give your seedlings and new plantings the follow-up water they need until winter's rains return.

Bring Garden Trimmings Inside

The holidays give us an excuse to make something festive out of our garden clippings. Deck the halls with boughs of holly-leaf cherry (*Prunus ilicifolia*). In many gardens, it grows well alongside bay (*Umbellularia californica*) and toyon (*Heteromeles arbutifolia*). All will hold up well through the holidays in a spray, a garland, or a wreath.

To make a simple spray, use florist's wire to secure stems of foliage together to create a full bouquet. Tuck in a cascade of red toyon berries collected from your garden, and tie a ribbon around the bundle and into a pretty bow. For a simple garland, connect overlapping lengths of another lovely evergreen, wax myrtle (*Myrica californica*), with wire and ribbon, and adorn it with the puffy little globes of common snowberry (*Symphoricarpos albus*).

California's native conifers are at home in the most traditional wreaths. To make one, start with a wreath base. You can construct it from lengths of denuded vine, such as California wild grape (*Vitis californica*) or virgin's bower (*Clematis ligusticifolia*), or from a coat hanger or other wire, or you can buy one. Fill out the wreath base with fragrant stems of redwood, pine, cedar, juniper, or fir. Take cuttings that are about eight inches long. Bundle groups of several cuttings together with wire to make little green posies, and trim the needles from the bottom two inches to make the posies easy to push into the wreath form. Tuck the first one into the wreath base, and let the stems follow the curve of the wreath. Secure the end of a spool of florist's wire to the wreath base at the same point, and firmly coil the wire around the posy to hold it in place. Place the next posy so that its foliage overlaps the base of the first, and so that it, too, follows the curve of the wreath, and continue to coil the wire securely. Go on overlapping the posies densely and coiling the wire securely until the wreath base is thickly and beautifully covered. Adorn it with clusters of pinecones or berries, or bells and a ribbon.

The custom of hanging evergreen wreaths in December dates back to at least the Roman Empire. It has been adapted ever since using different plants around the world. The use of California's conifers, bay, wax myrtle, and toyon is now customary here, but our native gardens offer many other possibilities. Live oak (*Quercus* spp.) provides both evergreen foliage and acorn and gall decorations. The green leaves and ruddy stems of manzanita (*Arctostaphylos* spp.) combine evergreen and embellishment in one. Holly-leaf cherry (*Prunus ilicifolia*), coffeeberry (*Rhamnus californica*), and sugar bush (*Rhus ovata*) are other good, long-lasting options that might be combined with rosehips or the leaves of Oregon grape (*Berberis* spp.). With just a few shrubs and trees in your own native garden, you are likely to have the materials you need for a long-lasting, beautiful wreath.

WHAT'S IN BLOOM?

Follow an Anna's hummingbird to find the classic December blooms in a native garden. You might see the hummingbird fly to the pink-white bells of a common manzanita (*Arctostaphylos manzanita*), the rosy pendants

The blooms of woodland strawberries mingle with the feathery leaves of poppy seedlings. HELEN POPPER

of a chaparral currant (*Ribes malvaceum*), or the brilliant red blooms of a fuchsia-flowered gooseberry (*R. speciosum*). Common manzanita hails from the northern part of the state, while chaparral currant and fuchsia-flowered gooseberry come from the south. All three flowering shrubs brighten gardens during the shortest days of the year.

December's garden also brings a sneak preview of the flowers of spring. Where annuals were sown early, we might see the first sunny faces of goldfields (*Lasthenia californica*), and—in some years—milkmaids (*Cardamine californica,* formerly *Dentaria laciniata*) and buttercups (*Ranunculus californicus*). Perennials, too, bring a taste of spring. Blue-eyed grass (*Sisyrinchium bellum*) forms pockets of cheer with little blue flowers, and both woodland and beach strawberry (*Fragaria vesca* and *F. chiloensis*)

Twinberry dangles
overhead. RENATE KEMPF

modestly open small white blooms. The flowers of fetid adder's tongue (*Scoliopus bigelovii*) evoke the tropics and lend an eerie drama to a moist woodland garden.

It is not only traditional blooms that grace the native garden now. Colorful berries, branches, and leaves combine in a subtle winter charm. Toyon shows off its large red berry clusters. Snowberry (*Symphoricarpos albus*) gives us little white globes. The polished orbs of coffeeberry (*Rhamnus californica*) ripen from mahogany to dark chocolate. Creek dogwood (*Cornus sericea*) displays vivid red stems. Stalwart leaves tarry on the sycamore (*Platanus racemosa*), maple (*Acer* spp.), California wild grape (*Vitis californica*), and spicebush (*Calycanthus occidentalis*). We can enjoy them right through the year's end.

DECEMBER

53

January

January is our wettest month. Much of California gets several inches of rain. In the wettest areas, the scarcity of pleasant, dry days may force you to pick and choose your chores. You may decide to prune winter deciduous plants along with a few perennials. In some cases, say with grape, this will be especially fun: *prune* will mean *take cuttings*. You'll finish the job with something to give your friends. In other cases, there's still just time to hack back the most vigorous growers, like established Matilija poppy (*Romneya coulteri*, fondly called frenzied fried egg) and California fuchsia (*Epilobium* spp.). Cuttings or no, your reward will be a more beautiful garden.

In unusual years, you may find that watering—of all things—is your surprise gardening activity this month. It is not likely to be a big chore, but it is important to watch

❮ Beach strawberry and blue-eyed grass provide groundcover. SAXON HOLT

JANUARY'S JOBS

Fake the rain

Many California garden plants need water now. If it doesn't come from the sky, get it from the spigot.

Prune

This is an excellent month to prune winter deciduous shrubs and small trees, as well as a few perennials. Many deciduous plants have lost their leaves and are still dormant, and there's little new growth yet on some perennials.

Propagate with cuttings

This is the fun part of that pruning.

Plant and sow

Where it's not too cold or soggy, most nursery plants will still do well if put in the ground now. For annual seeds, some of us successfully continue to sow them any old time.

Fertilize?

Few natives need fertilizer, but if stressed trees need it, this is a good time to give it to them.

Control pests

Watch out for beetle infestations of oaks (*Quercus* spp.) and tanoaks (*Lithocarpus densiflorus*). Use chicken wire to protect young plants from squirrels, rabbits, and deer.

Weed

If you can tell it's a weed, pull it.

for in a dry year. Skipping watering in a dry January might leave you disappointed both with the products of your recent plantings and with February's flowers. If a few weeks go by without rain, be sure to water your soon-to-be bloomers and your sensitive seedlings.

NATIVE GARDENING IN JANUARY

Fake the Rain

While most well-established natives can take a few dry weeks, newly planted natives can wither and die in unseasonably dry weather, particularly if it's windy. You may have planted some delicious woodland strawberry (*Fragaria vesca*) in fall, or maybe some bunchgrass or buckwheat (*Eriogonum* spp.). Friends have repeated, "Plant in the fall, to take advantage of still-warm soils and the coming rainy season." That's usually right, but there are dry spells. Most California natives—even the chaparral plants—need water until they are established, and nearly all of them expect water in January. If they don't get any from Mother Nature, give it to them from the garden hose.

Prune

Dormancy is a good overall guide to the timing of pruning. If winter deciduous plants, such as snowberry (*Symphoricarpos* spp.), rose (*Rosa* spp.), or elderberry (*Sambucus* spp.), need pruning, it's best done in winter. The ideal time is after they have lost their leaves. California wild grape (*Vitis californica*) is a happy reminder of this practice. Its colorful fall foliage is a cue to enjoy the last of its leaves, then prune.

Pruning is an art, and one approach is to act like a deer, nature's notorious pruner. Clip off the young tasty bits. This "mock deer" approach works particularly well for helping to maintain tree-like shrubs, including redbud (*Cercis occidentalis*). It's always a good idea to consider pruning oaks when they are young, so you can use clippers (and the mock-deer approach) rather than a chainsaw. Most deciduous oaks can be pruned now, but for evergreen oaks, wait until summer, when beetles and fungus are less active.

Few of California's natives take well to shearing, but many shrubs and small trees are improved by selective pruning. You may want to prune to remove crossing branches, keep walkways clear, or open up the plant to let in light and expose a shrub's "bones." Remove any deadwood, then take a good look at the plant. If you still think a branch needs to be removed, follow the branch down until you find an appropriate junction to cut back to. If it's possible, pull aside the offending branch to get a view of what the plant's structure would be without the branch. If you're happy with your imagined cut, use clean, sharp tools to make the actual cut a smooth one.

You can be ruthless with some plants. In addition to the perennials mentioned on page 46, common snowberry (*Symphoricarpos albus*) benefits from being cut back dramatically every few years or so. January is a good time to do this, before the surge of spring growth. Many perennials perform best when they are cut back hard every year. If you haven't already cut back established California fuchsia (*Epilobium* spp.), you can mow it now. It will return more stunning then ever. Yarrow (*Achillea millefolium*) may benefit from string trimming if it is growing out of bounds. Poverty weed (*Iva hayesiana*) also rejuvenates well after being cut back hard. Matilija poppy (*Romneya coulteri*) should be cut down to a foot high each year. It storms right back.

While some plants can take that ruthless pruning now, others cannot. Leave most woody chaparral plants, such as ceanothus (*Ceanothus* spp.) and manzanita (*Arctostaphylos* spp.), alone for now. Cutting them back during the rainy season would expose them to fungal disease. Instead, take your cue from their near dormancy in summer. Wait until then if they need shaping.

Propagate with Cuttings

January is a period of dormancy or slow growth for some plants. This makes it a good month to take cuttings. Propagating from cuttings now means there's not much going on to compete with root growth. You can take cuttings from dormant deciduous plants this month, making them hardwood cuttings. Or you can take them from evergreens, and they will be semi-hardwood cuttings. The hardwood cuttings are the easiest to keep alive since they lose no water through foliage. Prepare your cuttings as described on pages 35–37.

Below are some favorite garden plants that have been successfully propagated with January cuttings.

Coyote bush (*Baccharis pilularis*). Take semi-hardwood cuttings now that the flowering period is over. Coyote bush is quick to establish itself in the North Coast Ranges and into part of the South Coast Ranges. It is one of the first native plants to take over disturbed areas, such as road cuts and new developments. Plant it instead of the ubiquitous suburban box hedge. Or plant the low-growing variety *B. pilularis* 'Pigeon Point' for a bright green swath to cover a slope. This is a good plant to give your friends.

Grape (*Vitis californica*). This fast-growing plant roots easily from cuttings and is another good one for sharing. It is quite vigorous and will cover an arbor in just a few years. Vigorous as it is, it nevertheless can work in a small space. Grape can scramble quickly over a fence and trellis to give a tiny urban garden, hemmed in by a parking lot, a secluded feel in spring and summer. Some new, named varieties are more subdued.

Island snapdragon (*Galvezia speciosa*). This rare little evergreen shrub from the Channel Islands has "firecracker red" flowers nearly all year. If you have one, this is a good month to propagate it from stem cuttings.

Manzanita (*Arctostaphylos* spp.). California's many manzanitas thrive in infertile, well-drained soil. Cuttings are susceptible to rot, so take them from the somewhat hard growth from the previous season. The low-growing species are said to be the easiest to root, and the easiest of all is kinnikinnick (*A. uva-ursi*). Kinnikinnick stays close to the ground and drapes beautifully over retaining walls and other ledges. It does best in coastal or mountain gardens.

Mulefat (*Baccharis salicifolia*). While mulefat is not a tidy garden plant, it is an excellent wildlife plant and it is good for stabilizing streambeds, particularly in the southern part of the state. It grows easily from stout, long cuttings that are placed directly in moist soil.

Toyon (*Heteromeles arbutifolia*). January is the last good month for taking cuttings of this evergreen berry producer, which teems with red berries in winter. It is said to be the "holly" that covered the hills of Hollywood, giving the town its name.

Willow (*Salix* spp.). Willow is generally easy to root. While serious horticulturalists will use rooting hormone, home gardeners often skip both the hormone and the potting stage. They take large cuttings (long and thick) and put them right into their intended new home, where they can grow to stabilize a creek bed or provide a robust tromping ground for children and wildlife.

Plant and Sow

January is a good time to put more container plants into the ground in mild-winter areas. The air is still cool and moist, so small roots have little risk of drying out. Many plants establish themselves well now. Native gardeners can claim particular success planting a number of evergreen trees in January, including conifers, such as giant sequoia (*Sequoiadendron giganteum*) and incense-cedar (*Calocedrus decurrens*), and broad-leaf evergreens, such as holly-leaf cherry (*Prunus ilicifolia*). Giant sequoia takes space and time, but it tolerates drought and cold better than the state's coastal redwood (*Sequoia sempervirens*). Incense-cedar is a naturally symmetric, stately tree. It is aptly named for its fragrance and is suitable for a large formal garden. Despite being at home in the mountains, it tolerates some heat and drought. In dry woodland and chaparral gardens, holly-leaf cherry grows to be an elegant small tree. Most admired for its glossy foliage, it also bears clusters of white flowers that are followed by fruit that is attractive to birds. You can use it as a hedge, but it does drop its fruit, so think twice about planting it next to a sidewalk or patio. Plant it where the fruit and birds are welcome.

Nearly all natives can be planted in winter, and some can be planted anytime. Alders (*Alnus* spp.), those lovely deciduous trees, are among this group. You can put an alder in a lawn and treat it like a big birch tree (*Betula* spp.). It will enjoy the water. Annuals can also be sown now. Baby blue-eyes (*Nemophila menziesii*) are easy. Just broadcast them in moist soil and lightly scuff them in. Then make sure they have water when they are still tiny.

Fertilize?

Most of California's natives do better without fertilizer. The biggest kick from most fertilizers comes from nitrogen, and many of our natives evolved in nitrogen-poor soils. More nitrogen often just helps fast-growing weeds, not California's steadier natives. Fertilizers can rush native growth at the expense of flowers and longevity. Overuse of fertilizer also can disrupt the beneficial relationship between the plants' roots and the other organisms in the soil. Instead of fertilizing, you might mulch. Use organic (plant-based) mulches for woodland plants that are accustomed to leaf litter and gravel for plants that evolved in chaparral and desert regions. Organic mulch will eventually provide nutrients. Both mulches will help keep soil and moisture in place, and they will keep gardens looking nice. That said, there are conditions that occasionally call for fertilizer, such as for container plants or when evergreen trees are under stress, and January is a reasonable time for its use.

While dudleya and stonecrop do not rely on fertilizer when in the ground, they might benefit from it when grown in containers. HELEN POPPER

Control Pests

Some pests are serious, some aren't. Sometimes it's worth tolerating them. Sometimes it's not. Here's the range of pests likely to show themselves in January, along with some thoughts on how you might deal with them.

Ants and aphids. When you are out watering new plants, watch for Argentine ants (common house ants). In the smallest gardens, you can keep ants under control with repeated blastings of a strong jet from the hose. For serious infestations, bait stations may be needed. Where you see the ants, you often find aphids. Some blasts of water are often enough to take care of them as well. Take the trouble to hose them down now. Aphid problems worsen with new spring growth.

Beetles. A beetle infestation is serious in oaks and tanoaks. Bark beetles and ambrosia beetles spread a fungus that quickly kills even established trees. If a tree has dark, oozing patches or white sawdust-like frass, it may be infested with beetles. Consult a reputable arborist, because a progressive infestation is problematic. The disease can spread even if the infected tree is cut down.

Deer. Put chicken wire around and over young plants to protect them from deer. Some of the plants that deer don't normally eat will be eaten when the deer are hungry or when the plants are young. Deer are strong, so the chicken wire must be well secured.

Snails and slugs. These pests mean trouble for native seedlings, just as they do for nonnatives. Home remedies generally call for an enticement to lure snails and slugs into a container that they cannot get out of. A common trap is a saucer of beer (or yeast, sugar, and water), placed in a depression in the soil, but something more the size of a yogurt container will ensure the snails and slugs don't get out. Other "traps" are simply upside-down pots or raised boards, under which the creatures will hide. Simply turn the pots or boards over and dispose of the pests. After ridding snails and slugs from an enclosed area, such as a raised bed, some gardeners use copper barriers to keep the pests out. Still others rely on oak or gravel mulch to keep them at bay. Those who take them more seriously use poisons containing iron phosphate (not metaldehyde, which is poisonous to other wildlife and to pets) around the seedlings. In gardens with a scarcity of water and a plethora of birds, snails and slugs are not much of a problem.

Squirrels and rabbits.   You might think it is the pesky deer that are eating your young plants, but the damage from squirrels and rabbits looks much the same. Chicken wire will protect your young, susceptible plants from them too.

Weed

Weeding is an important January job because early weeding means less weeding overall. January is also an easy time to dig up weeds because the newly sprouted weeds are small and the soil is soft. Knowing that weeds are hard to recognize and difficult to eradicate, some gardeners pull up any seedlings that they haven't intentionally sown. This includes some native annuals that begin to establish themselves in the wrong place. Poppies (*Eschscholzia californica*) and miner's lettuce (*Claytonia perfoliata*), for example, are so prolific that after a few years, you might just till them under when you see them coming up (though they never pose a real problem, and a bumper crop of miner's lettuce gives you something to bring to friends). Each year of weeding makes it easier to distinguish the troublesome weeds from the sprouts of beloved native annuals. In

In this selection of weeds from the author's garden, notice the tiny, troublesome bulblets on the sourgrass, pictured in the center. Detached and left behind, these will bring yet more weeds. HELEN POPPER

63

the meantime, remember that weeds are always volunteers, so treat the volunteers as suspect.

WHAT'S IN BLOOM?

Manzanita (*Arctostaphylos* spp.) is the star of January's garden. Its red bark glistens in the rain, and clusters of white or pink-white bells hang delicately from the tips of its branches. Hummingbirds hover below the bells to feed.

The flowers of currants and gooseberries (*Ribes* spp.) provide more nectar for hummingbirds, while silk-tassels (*Garrya elliptica*) show off the long, decorative catkins that give them their common name. Currants and gooseberries begin blooming in the southern part of the state,

Manzanita brings early blooms. WILDSCAPING.COM

then extend their display northward. The blooms of pink-flowering currants (*Ribes sanguineum*) hang in heavy panicles. Pink chaparral currants (*R. malvaceum*) often bloom now too, though they can begin as early as November. The fire-engine red blooms of fuchsia-flowering gooseberries (*R. speciosum*) dangle densely in rows along spine-covered branches, standing out vibrantly against glossy green leaves. As a shrub, gooseberries have something of the overall look of flowering quince (*Chaenomeles* spp., all nonnative), though the gooseberries' flowers themselves are tubular.

Hummingbird sage (*Salvia spathacea*) can be another source of winter nectar. It thrives with leaf litter or mulch. Once established, it sends up tall stalks carrying whorls of magenta blooms. The very earliest of these begin to open for the hummingbirds, and for us, after New Year's Day.

Hummingbird sage provides nectar for its namesake. JUDY KRAMER

Clean and Weed

February

It's still officially winter, even here in California. Many of us spend most of our February gardening hours preparing for the oncoming rush of spring. February is the month to step outside and clean up what has accumulated over much of winter—including tree branches that have fallen in the wrong place during our storms—so that spring flowers and new growth will look their best. Now is the ideal time to prune some of the shrubs that have already flowered, such as gooseberries (*Ribes speciosum*). It is also a good time to clean up many of the perennials that have gotten tattered over the winter.

Weeding begins in earnest this month, starting with the most aggressive early germinators. To help keep weeds (and mud—after all, it is still the rainy season in most of the state) under control, add mulch. In addition to helping

◀ Manzanita, ceanothus, and redbud bloom together at Rancho Santa Ana. SAXON HOLT

FEBRUARY'S JOBS

Clean up after the storms

Whether it's fallen branches or fallen retaining walls, take stock of what needs to be cleaned up. Some branches and leaf litter can be left for wildlife habitat. Other storm leavings should be cleaned up, both to prevent future hazards and to keep them from harming delicate young plants.

Mulch

Top off mulch. This will keep down the muddy mess when it's wet and help retain moisture for thirsty plants when it's not.

Prune

Cut back the dead portions of perennials that have become rangy, so they'll be ready for new growth, but don't cheat yourself out of blooms by pruning plants that have already set their buds. Avoid pruning woody chaparral shrubs now—save that for summer.

Propagate

Take cuttings from evergreen shrubs while there is new growth and no flowers, and from deciduous ones before buds set. This is also a good time to layer viney, flexible plants.

Sow seeds

Broadcast seeds for spring annuals. Mix some dirt with the tiniest seeds, then rake or simply scuff them in.

Control pests

Check for slugs, snails, and earwigs.

Water only if it's needed

Water seedlings and young plants during extended dry spells.

Weed

Weed out the aggressive early germinators that follow every rain. Look for sourgrass (*Oxalis pes-caprae*), European grasses, and French and Scotch broom (*Genista monspessulana* and *Cytisus scoparius*).

keep the weeds and mud at bay, the mulch will provide a uniform back-drop to the showy new spring growth, making it stand out beautifully in the months to come.

All this preparation for spring draws us outside to enjoy California's precocious bloomers and the wildlife that goes with them, including the beautiful bells of the manzanitas and their winged admirers, the hummingbirds.

NATIVE GARDENING IN FEBRUARY
Clean Up after the Storms

February is a month for good garden grooming. Pick up hazardous branches that the wind and water may have knocked down. Inspect trees for additional threatening limbs. Walk around and take a peek at manmade garden structures and ornaments. Check for labels you may have carefully tucked in around your fall seedlings. Did the storms knock them down or blow them away? Have things tipped over, cracked, or come loose? Assess damage to fences, retaining walls, and walkways. Repair or replace what is still needed.

Now, if you are a particularly tidy gardener (and if the wind hasn't already done this job for you), you can add a bit of drama to your earliest spring-flowering shrubs by pulling off the spent leaves in the beginning of the month. Flowers that emerge on bare stems are particularly striking.

Mulch

February's good garden grooming continues with mulch. Mulch helps in the battle against weeds, it keeps down the mud during wet spells, and it keeps moisture in the soil during dry spells. It also provides a nice visual backdrop for the fresh spring growth that is on its way. This is also a good time to top off mulch on paths, where it not only keeps the mud down but staves off erosion.

As you mulch, be careful not to compact the wet soil in planting areas. You may want to forgo mulch where you have sown wildflower seeds that have not germinated. Few are robust enough to grow through heavy mulch. Where bulbs are just coming up, mulch with a light hand.

There are many types of mulch, including wood, bark, leaves, and gravel. Which type is best depends on the garden's style and, most important, the mix of plants. In a woodland garden—where many of the plants evolved in a setting rich in leaf litter—redwood, pine, and oak mulch is great. For oak woodlands and plants with a more Mediterranean feel, organic (woody) mulch can be mixed with rocks or gravel. For plants that evolved in the relatively nutrient-poor chaparral, organic mulch should be used much more sparingly. Rocks and gravel feed neither weeds nor fires.

Oak leaves provide mulch to keep down weeds, but the leaves should be pulled off the low-growing Hearst's ceanothus (*Ceanothus hearstiorum*) for it to look its best.
STEPHEN INGRAM

Keep in mind that mulches differ in their ability to hold moisture. While wood chips hold moisture, sawdust and overly fine bark can shed it. If your mulch seems to shed water, make sure the water gets under the mulch, and add mulch only after watering. Soaker hoses under mulch work well. Few of our natives are adapted to constant moisture, so in most garden settings mulch should dry out between warm-weather waterings. Warm, moist soil harbors fungal pathogens, so it is important to keep mulch away from a plant's trunk or root crown.

Some woodland gardens use a combination of mulches. In the more formal parts of many gardens, redwood bark and pine chippings, perhaps from locally fallen trees, are appropriate. The redwood, in particular, provides a finished look and seems to last a good long time. Fine versions of redwood bark work especially well around ferns, western columbines (*Aquilegia formosa*), western azaleas (*Rhododendron occidentale*), and the most delicate redwood understory plants. If your garden includes oaks, then you can collect some of their leaves to use as mulch in other parts of your garden. Collected oak leaves provide an attractive, unfussy cover. They stop many weeds, and they keep the way open and inviting in the most informal of garden paths.

In this sunny chaparral garden, gravel mulch provides a path between beds of poppies and sage.
HELEN POPPER

You might also consider the "other mulches": plants and rocks. Both can help keep weeds down and control erosion. If your garden soil is punctuated by rocks, grab those when you come across them and toss them into a pile. You can use them later in an area where they will do some good in keeping the weeds down and the soil in place. If you have recently cleared your garden of an expanse of weeds, then you are likely to have exposed a swath of bare dirt. There, mulch becomes especially important: the bare dirt is a magnet for all the weedy seeds of the neighborhood. One way to preempt their establishment is to cover the dirt with something else. In some places, standard mulch might be just the thing. In others, rocks are effective and attractive. The rocks that came from elsewhere in your garden, the vernacular ones, are likely to be the most attractive. For the remaining areas, sow fast-germinating seeds—natives that will out-compete the weeds. Poppies (*Eschscholzia californica*) are especially good for this. They are easy-germinating, fast-growing plants, and they are easy to keep under control after they've taken hold.

Once your native garden begins to get established, you'll find weeds to be less of a problem, particularly in the garden's drier quarters. The garden will begin to provide its own mulch in roughly the right quantities, and mulching will become a small job, perhaps just entailing moving leaf litter from one area of the garden to another. Most native gardeners want to let some of the earth show itself again. Bare earth provides a home for beneficial ground-nesting insects, including native bees. (The Urban Bee Project at the University of California at Berkeley provides advice for bee-friendly gardening.) Even the most fastidious gardeners can welcome some of these dwellers with open-air patches of earth under or behind maturing shrubs. Not only does the established native garden begin to take mulching work out of your hands, it begins to host its own pollinators.

Prune (and Don't Prune)

Many perennials and groundcovers that haven't been cut back yet are looking tatty right now. That serves as a gentle reminder to prune them. Not only will your garden look better now, but the plant itself will perform better when its new growth explodes in spring. If you haven't already mowed back your established California fuchsias (*Epilobium* spp.)

and Matilija poppies (*Romneya coulteri*), do it this month. Yarrow (*Achillea millefolium*) and some of the perennial sages (*Salvia* spp.) are likely to need a good cleaning up by now as well. There is also still time to prune deciduous trees, shrubs, or vines that linger in dormancy. For a wildlife garden, leave some of the clipped brush, perhaps in a strategically placed pile, to provide a desirable habitat.

As coyote bush (*Baccharis pilularis*) ages, its branches can begin to look bare, with growth only at their tips. While this exposed, sculptural look is appealing in some, it doesn't fit most gardens. To rejuvenate coyote bush, coppice or cut it back hard in winter, almost to its base. Spring will renew the plant with fresh growth.

Many perennials benefit from a little trimming back. This inviting chair remains inviting when the—true to its name—prickly phlox (*Leptodactylon californicum*) is kept off the seat. WILDSCAPING.COM

With just a few exceptions, it's best not to prune woody chaparral plants now. Instead, wait until summer to prune them when they are closer to being dormant. And if when walking out among your plants you see some that are already setting buds, keep your clippers in your pocket and pass them by. Wait a bit and use the clippers another time, when your light pruning will reward you with sprigs of flowers to bring back into the house with you. Seeing buds on ceanothus (*Ceanothus* spp.) now, you can anticipate a fragrant sachet of clippings if you wait.

Propagate

PROPAGATE FROM THICKETS Some plants are naturals for propagation right now, and they show it. Oregon grape, for example (*Berberis aquifolium,* also called *Mahonia aquifolium*), has a habit of forming root suckers and tends to make a large thicket of clones. The root suckers have pretty yellow stems with yellow roots already attached. Take some of the suckers with ample roots and you're on your way to starting a new clump. Be careful where you start one. The leaves of the Oregon grape are not supple like true grape leaves; instead, they're a bit prickly. This makes the plant nice as a background plant, and even nicer as a barrier plant, but less nice when situated near other plants that require handling.

Other *Berberis* species—from the shade-loving long-leaf barberry (*Berberis nervosa*) of conifer forests to Nevin's barberry (*Berberis nevinii*), which can handle the desert—can be propagated the same way. So can many other sucker-forming shrubs, such as common snowberry (*Symphoricarpos albus*), Matilija poppy (*Romneya coulteri*), wild mock orange (*Philadelphus lewisii*), and Douglas' spirea (*Spiraea douglasii*).

PROPAGATE FROM CUTTINGS Cuttings can be taken now from many evergreen shrubs, like coyote bush (*Baccharis pilularis*), while there is semi-hard new growth and no flowers. There also is still just time to take hardwood cuttings before buds set on deciduous plants, such as the California dogwood (*Cornus californica*). Prepare them as described on pages 35–37.

PROPAGATE BY LAYERING February is a good time to propagate by layering. Layering is a cinch on viney, flexible plants. Nick a bottom branch away from the center of the plant, then (perhaps using rooting hormone—there is some controversy here) simply bury the nicked portion of the branch. Later, roots will form, making it a new plant that can be carefully cut out and moved during any cool, wet month. Some manzanitas, such as kinnikinnick (*Arctostaphylos uva-ursi*), are good candidates for layering. Kinnikinnick can remain vigorous for decades, and layering takes advantage of its naturally trailing branches. Short stretches of the trailing branches can be buried easily now and removed in fall if new roots form. Many mat-forming perennials layer themselves. In that case, propagation simply entails cutting out a section of the perennial "carpet" and moving it to begin anew somewhere else in the garden.

Sow Seeds

In February we near the tail end of the fall and winter sowing season. Seeds sown earlier will produce large plants and generally showier flowers. However, sowing additional seeds now will extend the garden's bloom period. Sowing is simple and it's gratifying now, when the days are longer and the shoots seem to grow more quickly. Some gardeners say you'll have the best chance of beating the birds if you go out into the garden just before a forecast of two or three days of rain.

Two of the most successful and most spectacular spring-blooming native wildflowers whose seeds you can sow now are elegant clarkia (*Clarkia unguiculata*) and, of course, our state flower, the California poppy (*Eschscholzia californica*). Elegant clarkia is tall and yields nice cutting flowers, while the familiar poppy has a mound of pretty, airy foliage and abundant brilliant orange or yellow flowers. With both rainfall and increasing warmth, there's still time for either of them to take off and bloom well in late spring.

Sow the seeds in a sunny spot with "poor" soil. Go outside with a bit of seed in a bowl, pick up a handful of dirt, and mix the seeds with it. Then just sprinkle the mixture where you want the flowering plants to grow. If it's not too muddy, you might stomp or scuff it in a bit; some say this helps protect the seeds from the birds. More careful gardeners sow annuals in six-packs in the greenhouse to avoid losses to birds. Others have good luck sowing directly, which is, of course, the easy way.

This is one of the jobs that is fun enough (and short enough) to lure us—perhaps with children—out to enjoy a fine mist or light rain in the garden. You might find yourself staying out longer and getting wetter than you expected, attacking weeds or moving branches, but so much the better.

Control Pests

Check for slugs and small snails, which can munch your seedlings down to the dirt. Mulching and weeding help on this front. The open mulch exposes the slugs and snails to equally voracious birds. Beware of bait pellets, which are noxious to earthworms and dogs. Also, watch to see what is eating your plants. Is it snails or earwigs? For earwigs, roll up some newspaper and leave it outside. The earwigs will crawl in, and then you can dispose of them.

Look for ants on shrubs and small trees. In the mild-winter areas of the state, if you find ants, you may also find aphids. You can blast both away with a hose. If they're attacking, say, a young California bay laurel (*Umbellularia californica*), you might try a combination of cutting away the worst-infected area and blasting the rest with water. That will work well if the infestation is mild. Some gardeners use insecticidal soap, but blasting them off with the hose is the quickest way.

Water Only if It's Needed

Attend to any of those rare extended (and often windy) dry spells. Your littlest seedlings and new plantings are expecting water, and they'll need water from you if it doesn't rain. Otherwise, let nature take its course.

Weed

Sourgrass (*Oxalis pes-caprae*, also known as Bermuda buttercup and buttercup oxalis) comes in thickly now if its little shoots weren't dug up when they first showed themselves. This pretty, pesky weed is difficult to eradicate. If it's new to your garden, work now to make sure it doesn't establish itself. Don't let it continue to grow—that feeds the little bulb lying six inches or so below the surface. Gardeners who have successfully overcome an established oxalis colony have combined aggressive weeding with heavy mulch (sometimes layers of newspaper), chickens, or, in some cases, chemicals. If there is just a bit of it, it is worth the effort to keep it at bay by weeding, and by following up with more weeding.

As far as the less troublesome weeds go, this is a good month to go after them too, even unwanted volunteers of otherwise pleasant plants. Pull them now, while the ground is soft and the pulling is easy.

WHAT'S IN BLOOM?

Going out into the garden on a cool or misty February day, you might admire the vivid blue sprays of Ray Hartman ceanothus (*Ceanothus* 'Ray Hartman'), which is lovely and easy to find in nurseries. Its early blooms are a bit of a surprise. Ray Hartman is a cross between an island ceanothus (*C. arboreus*) and a Carmel ceanothus (*C. griseus*), both of which

Enjoy the buds and flowers of Point Reyes ceanothus (*Ceanothus gloriosus*). The plants can be pinched back to keep them full when the blooms are finished.

STEPHEN INGRAM

typically bloom later. Also in show now is pink-flowering currant (*Ribes sanguineum*), with its softly draping rosy clusters. Manzanita (*Arctostaphylos* spp.) continues to delight us with its delicate, urn-shaped flowers.

Down at our feet, and promising future sweetness, are the tiny white blossoms of woodland strawberries (*Fragaria vesca*). Other blooming woodland plants include wakerobins (*Trillium chloropetalum* and *T. ovatum*), largeflower fairybells (*Prosartes smithii*), milkmaids (*Cardamine californica*), and the first of the western columbines (*Aquilegia formosa*). Out in the sun, we already find many garden-friendly wildflowers, such as Menzies' wallflowers (*Erysimum menziesii*), peppermint candy flowers (*Claytonia sibirica*), and nearly everyone's favorite, diminutive baby blue-eyes (*Nemophila menziesii*). Yes, it's officially still winter, but don't tell the wildflowers.

Wakerobins grace an urban garden. PAUL FURMAN

Spring Anew

March

Most of us in California live in mild-winter areas, and we planted and sowed the seeds of natives in fall and early winter. Now, the last serious threat of hard frost—if there ever was one—disappears. March brings warmer weather, Arbor Day, and the official arrival of spring to spur us on. In these mild-winter areas, we may be swept up in a second wave of planting.

Others of us live in areas with voracious fall browsers and hard winter freezes. Taught by experience and by our friends, we don't plant in fall. Instead, we bide our time, waiting for the cold to pass and for the deer to find nibbling options outside our gardens. In these areas, we plant in spring.

❮ Tansy-leaf phacelia and Tilden Park ceanothus bloom in an appealing front garden.
HELEN POPPER

MARCH'S JOBS

Celebrate Arbor Day

In your garden, in schools and parks, and on the street, plant and protect native trees.

Sow annuals for summer bloom

While fall sowing yields California's showy spring wildflower displays, spring sowing will extend the blooming period through summer and even early fall.

Weed

Weed now, while young weeds haven't set seed and are easy to pull.

Plant

If you garden in cold-winter areas, plant as soon as the threat of serious frost is over. In mild-winter areas, plant anything that will continue to get water during summer.

Propagate

Divide moisture-loving plants now.

Prune

Pinch back ceanothus (*Ceanothus* spp.), coffeeberry (*Rhamnus californica*), and manzanita (*Arctostaphylos* spp.) if you would like a leafier look. Shape deciduous plants that haven't leafed out yet if they need it. You can also coppice a few amenable older shrubs to rejuvenate them now.

Tidy up

Add mulch where it's lean. Clean and sharpen tools. Use your now-sharp clippers to pick a posy to enjoy inside.

Water

If it doesn't rain, water seedlings, wildflowers, and summer-dry plants.

Whether it is our first wave of planting or our second, spring planting requires attention to the water supply. We can sow seeds during a fine rain, or we can gently water them in using a hose. We can plant from containers after rains have soaked the planting holes, or we can plant them after we have soaked the planting holes ourselves. Then we must continue to watch our new plantings closely and water them when needed.

NATIVE GARDENING IN MARCH
Celebrate Arbor Day

March brings Arbor Day to California. Celebrate it this month by admiring, sustaining, or—for some species—planting our beautiful native trees in your own garden. In *Growing California Native Plants,* Marjorie Schmidt thoughtfully describes dozens of native trees that populated gardens and avenues more than thirty years ago. Since then, even more species have been introduced to the horticultural trade. Contrary to the received wisdom a generation ago, native trees in all sizes and shapes now contend for garden space in every region of the state. Even the smallest garden has room for a large native shrub trained to show off as a patio tree. Most of them can be planted successfully on Arbor Day as long as they are given sufficient water through at least their first year.

CHERISH AN OAK Some of the best garden trees include our native oaks (*Quercus* spp.). California boasts twenty native oak species, and even more varieties. We have them on the coast and inland, deciduous and evergreen, large and small. Many gardeners can find a way to host this California icon. With a plan for careful monitoring of water needs through spring and the upcoming summer, oaks can be planted successfully now.

As you plant on Arbor Day, keep in mind that experienced California gardeners and horticulturists don't all agree on the optimal planting season for oaks. Some advise us to plant in fall, others say plant in early spring. Fans of fall planting usually hail from the mild-winter areas, where most Californians live. Mild winters provide fall-planted oaks with extra time to establish their roots before the rigors of summer arrive. Summer watering demands a careful balancing act. We must weigh the perils to young plants of scant summer rainfall against the increased threat of the fatal fungi that regular summer watering encourages. Knowing their roots have been growing since fall helps us steel ourselves against the seduction of overwatering our oaks in summer.

Spring planting aficionados remind us that fall planting has its disadvantages. First, in many areas it is followed by hard freezes, which can kill young plants. Freeze certainly trumps drought in California's harsh-winter areas, making spring planting the clear choice in the mountains and inner valleys where temperatures regularly drop down to the teens. Second, in many suburban and rural gardens, fall brings the hungriest mammals, especially deer. By early fall, local deer will have mowed down much of their usual habitat; they will become hungrier, more daring, and more destructive. Even species that are deer resistant when mature are vulnerable as seedlings to the voracious browsers.

While fall planting eases the summer water worry, spring planting mitigates extreme frost and deer concerns. Take your pick. But if you'd like an oak, don't hold back on Arbor Day. Whether or not it's the *best* day to plant, it's a good day to plant.

For those of us who already have an oak in our garden, we can cherish it on Arbor Day by removing any soil or mulch that may have built up around its trunk and root crown, by weeding under its canopy, and by leaving some leaf litter in place there. All the while, and after, we can enjoy the complex wildlife community it supports.

CONSIDER A MAPLE OR A SYCAMORE Trees that can tolerate—or need—summer moisture are excellent candidates for Arbor Day planting. If there will be regular access to summer water, you might consider a riparian species, such as one of California's maples (*Acer* spp.) or a western sycamore (*Platanus racemosa*). Neither needs constant moisture, but they do need it regularly.

The smallest maple, the vine maple (*A. circinatum*), grows slowly, but it is elegant even when young, with fine leaves and stunning fall color. It makes an excellent container specimen. Also beautiful in the fall, but more luxuriant than its exquisite little cousin, is the largest of our maples:

big-leaf maple (*A. macrophyllum*). True to both its common name and its Latin one, it has big leaves. Deeply lobed, the leaves take on the look of enormous hands, so big that they evoke the myth of Sasquatch. They emerge in spring with a bronze hue and mature in summer to a cheery green. In fall, they yellow brightly and linger to reflect the lowering sun. Planted now and given regular water, a big-leaf maple will grow speedily until cool weather arrives.

A sycamore grows quickly into a large, stately tree. Its white bark gleams in its own shade. With its peeling bark, parchment-like leaves, and spherical red female flowers, it is a child-pleasing tree. It also pleases wildlife, drawing in waxwings, woodpeckers, and kingbirds and providing a bit of down for hummingbirds to use in their nests. A fast grower, it often makes a good substitute for nonnative eucalyptus. In the wild, sycamores grow near water, and in the garden, they seek it out. So while a sycamore is not a good candidate for planting over a sewer line, it will tolerate being near a lawn. The tree might stretch out over the green with a great and sturdy horizontal limb—a high one to hold a swing, or a low one where friends can sit, dangling their feet and tickling their toes in the grass.

The leaves of maples emerge quickly in spring. Here, a big-leaf maple breaks dormancy. HELEN POPPER

FIT IN A SMALL TREE Many of us are thinking of planting something more modest on Arbor Day: a tree that will fit into a tiny garden, or even the courtyard of an office or school. To satisfy that desire now, the vine maple will certainly do, but you may also want to consider some of the natives on the margin between trees and shrubs. These include wax myrtle (*Myrica californica*) where there's water, redbud (*Cercis occidentalis*) where winters bring a chill, desert willow (*Chilopsis linearis*) or an upright variety of flannel bush (such as *Fremontodendron* 'Pacific Sunset') where summers come on strong, and flowering ash (*Fraxinus dipetala*) almost anywhere. The first three are amenable to pruning into sculptural, multi-trunked trees and are well suited to an urban landscape, and all are suitable for a postage-stamp wilderness. Wax myrtle has the added benefit of scented leaves; redbud heralds early spring with masses of magenta blooms; flannel bush follows with a bold display of cup-sized gold flowers; flowering ash provides scented blooms in spring; and desert willow blooms extravagantly in summer.

PLANT A NATIVE STREET TREE In many cities, Arbor Day reawakens a zeal for planting street trees. The best street trees are tidy, have well-behaved roots, leave room for pedestrians, and need little maintenance. Many urban foresters have begun to note the deficiencies of some of our nonnative street tree choices, including southern California's two most common street trees, liquidambar (*Liquidambar styraciflua*) and magnolia (*Magnolia* spp.). Both are notorious sidewalk lifters and litterers. More and more cities have come to recognize the good choices offered by natives.

The city of Los Angeles lists two dozen native trees suitable for planting in the public right of way, and native oak (*Quercus* spp.), California black walnut (*Juglans californica*), California bay (*Umbellularia californica*), and western sycamore (*Platanus racemosa*) are protected throughout the city. The city of Carmel explicitly favors the planting of natives and gives priority to the planting of three distinctive locals: Monterey pine (*Pinus radiata*), Monterey cypress (*Cupressus macrocarpa*), and coast live oak (*Quercus agrifolia*). Well inland, many cities have for decades lined their streets with natives, including white alder (*Alnus rhombifolia*), velvet ash (*Fraxinus velutina*), and northern California black walnut (*Juglans californica*). All three are graceful shade trees, and they tolerate clay soils. (The black walnut, however, does drop litter that suppresses many other plants.) The densest urban areas often need small street trees to fit in the cutouts of narrow parkways. The city of San Diego lists some excellent native choices for narrow confines: western redbud (*Cercis occidentalis*), mountain mahogany (*Cercocarpus betuloides*), toyon (*Heteromeles arbutifolia*), and Catalina ironwood (*Lyonothamnus floribundus*). All offer precious islands of habitat and beauty.

Sow Annuals for Summer Bloom

While the seeds of most native annuals are best sown in fall, many can be sown now. Wildflower enthusiasts often sow in fall for a spring show, then again in spring to extend the display into summer and sometimes a little longer. In most areas, spring sowing calls for supplemental water from beginning to end—first, regular water as the seedlings are just coming up; then intermittent water to keep the plants growing and blooming.

The best candidates for late or repeat sowing are those that are untroubled by the combination of warmth and at least occasional water. Luckily, these include some of our easiest germinators: California poppy (*Eschscholzia californica*, really a perennial); *Clarkia* species, especially elegant clarkia (*C. unguiculata*); and globe gilia (*Gilia capitata*). All three readily self-sow after just one season. Another easy one is sunflower (*Helianthus annuus*). Cultivated for its seed by Native Americans before European settlers arrived, this cheerful flower is the same species that is grown so familiarly alongside vegetable patches throughout the country. Other good candidates for spring sowing include bird's-eye gilia (*Gilia tricolor*) for dry, open areas, baby blue-eyes (*Nemophila menziesii*) where there'll be a bit more water, and Chinese houses (*Collinsia heterophylla*) for September blooms in dappled shade. All eventually establish themselves with self-sowing if they are allowed to go to seed.

Weed

March is a great time to weed. Many weeds are mature enough to be easily identifiable but not mature enough to set seed. You can start with a hoe for the youngest weeds, then hand-pull the others. Throughout much of the state, the soil is still soft enough that hand-pulling a weed will secure its entire root.

Be especially vigilant about French and Scotch broom (*Genista monspessulana* and *Cytisus scoparius*). Brooms usually invade sunny, newly tilled areas, but they also sneak up under the protection of young shrubs. They can shoot up three feet in the first year. If last year's brooms got away from you and you cannot get to their roots, then cut them down now. You are likely to kill about half of them that way, and you will prevent the remaining ones from setting seed this season. You will be glad you did: their seeds remain viable for years, sometimes decades.

Plant

In California's cold-winter regions, the time to put plants in the ground is when the chance of hard frost has diminished. In the coldest of these regions, it is still too cold to plant. In the mildest of them, the chance of hard frosts begins to abate in March, so gardeners can start to set out plants.

Spring plantings rejuvenate the native plants on the roof of the California Academy of Sciences in San Francisco. HELEN POPPER

For those of us who planted in fall but want more, this is a good time to plant anything that will receive summer water. It's an especially good time to plant along ponds and stream banks. As the rains die out, you might plant a torrent sedge (*Carex nudata*) in a stream bed or even in an irrigated part of the garden—anywhere that it won't completely dry out. Many gardeners also have had success planting perennial grasses now, or anytime it's not too hot.

Propagate

In the understory of California's moist, coniferous forests and riparian woodlands grow many garden-worthy plants that can be propagated now through division. If you have mature clumps of fairybells (*Prosartes hookeri* and *P. smithii*), false lily of the valley (*Maianthemum dilatatum*), white

insideout flower (*Vancouveria hexandra*), or Pacific bleeding heart (*Dicentra formosa*), divide them now if they are crowded or if you or your friends would like more of them. Divide them before substantial new growth begins.

If you have a high ledge or rock wall, try draping your new clumps of fairy bells over it to show off their delicate, bell-shaped flowers; or let them fill in behind western columbine (*Aquilegia formosa*) or coral bells (*Heuchera* spp.). Divide false lily of the valley and insideout to increase your groundcover in moist shade. Bring some of your newly divided Pacific bleeding hearts close to a shady path or seat, where you won't miss their sweet nodding blooms. With the prospect of moisture, other good candidates for division now include blue-eyed grass (*Sisyrinchium bellum*), sedges (*Carex* spp.), and rushes (*Juncus* spp.).

The less ambitious among us can skip making our own divisions and still have a shot at propagating woodland understory plants. Coral bells (*Heuchera* spp.) can be lazily propagated with stem cuttings (postpone dividing them until fall). Simply snap off a few woody stems, cut off any flowers, then poke the woody portions in the ground where you want them to grow. Experienced masters of lazy gardening techniques use this for an instant little native border. Woodland strawberry (*Fragaria vesca*), osoberry (*Osmaronia cerasiformis*), and common snowberry (*Symphoricarpos albus*) form natural divisions on their own: new, rooted sections that can be cut off and lifted out. If they will continue to receive at least some summer moisture, you can lift these self-made divisions and move them now.

Prune

Prune only with a clear intent. You might prune to promote flowering, to expose lower portions of the plant to light and admiration, to clean up a plant, to keep it within bounds, or to reinvigorate it. Then, whether you pinch, select, coppice, or mow, choose the pruning method that suits your purpose.

To make plants bushier, pinch back the tips of branches. Pinching is akin to light browsing by herbivores, and it promotes new growth from leaf buds that are left behind. It is helpful for shrubs that tend to push out their new growth at the far ends of their branches, beyond their flowers. Without pinching or browsing, the new growth leaves behind bare, woody stems. For leafier ceanothus (*Ceanothus* spp.), coffeeberry (*Rhamnus californica*), and manzanita (*Arctostaphylos* spp.), pinch them back after they have bloomed. Keep in mind, however, that too much leafiness impedes good air flow and shades a plant's lower leaves. For now, pinch back only small stems, the ones that are less than a quarter of an inch thick. (You can use them as cuttings.) You may follow later, in summer, with selective pruning of ceanothus, coffeeberry, and manzanita to keep their overall structures open. Wait for summer to prune your sages as well.

This month, you can selectively prune vigorous island morning glory (*Calystegia macrostegia*) if needed. Clean out dead material; then choose the vines you want to keep long and cut the others as far back as green, nonwoody growth allows. To maintain the characteristic shapes of lupines (*Lupinus* spp.) and pitcher sage (*Lepechinia,* not a true sage), cut them back now as well, by as much as half.

Several large shrubs also are ready for selective pruning. While you can shape wax myrtle (*Myrica californica*) now or any other time, early spring is a good time to prune some deciduous shrubs, such as creek dogwood (*Cornus sericea*), redbud (*Cercis occidentalis*), and desert willow (*Chilopsis linearis*). For drama next winter, cut back some of the older central canes of dogwood now. Its bright winter color is most intense on new canes. For basketry canes or for the most drama, you can cut all of the dogwood canes back to a foot or so; but the price of such hard pruning will be fewer leaves, flowers, and berries along the way. If you would like to contain the dogwood's growth, then remove its outermost suckers.

When pruning the redbud, take in some of the flower-covered branches to show them off. Or, if they haven't bloomed yet, give forcing a try. Fill a large, sturdy container with tepid water, then split or smash the branches' ends to allow them to take up water freely. Start them off in a cool spot, then place them prominently when they are ready to flaunt their blooms.

The most dramatic forms of pruning are coppicing and mowing. Reserve these techniques for established plants that might have relied successfully on fire in a natural setting. Like fire, coppicing and mowing take the plants right down to the ground, or nearly so. Consider coppicing for an old redbud that no longer blooms freely, for a semi-naked coyote bush with foliage only on its outer reaches, or for an over-tall elderberry. In order to make the most of spring growth, coppice coyote bush at the beginning of the month, or elderberry any time this month. (Wait for fall to coppice a redbud.) The buzz cut of pruning, coppicing can be as scary to the uninitiated as a first haircut can be to a small child. If you're reluctant to coppice, you can compromise a bit: space the process out, completing it over two or three years by selecting some branches to cut each year. Be sure to take out the dead or diseased wood first. As for mowing, you can cut back warm-season grasses, such as salt grass and deer grass (*Distichlis spicata* and *Muhlenbergia rigens*), now or anytime in spring for a soft look the rest of the year. If you plan to give these grasses a light fertilizer, give it to them now to fuel their return. Wait for the dormancy of late summer to clean up cool-season grasses.

Tidy Up

Depending on your own habits, you might want to spend a bit of time just strolling around the garden tidying up here and there. Repair a loose fence board; clean out a bird bath; locate, clean, sharpen, and store your tools where they will be handy. Top off mulch where it's needed.

The amount of mulch will depend on its function and type, and on your garden. While many mature native gardens eventually need no added mulch, heavy mulching is helpful when first establishing a native garden. For serious weed suppression in new woodland or riparian gardens, you might want six to ten inches of an arborist's chippings. In most areas, arborist chippings are delivered free in large amounts to your driveway. Use a trusted arborist to ensure that you don't get chippings of problem plants. Some chippings, such as those of diseased oaks or healthy bay trees, can carry *Phytophthora ramorum,* the pathogen that causes sudden oak death. (In San Diego County, all oaks must be chipped to one inch or less to avoid the risk of spreading a new pest, the gold-spotted oak borer.) Ask the arborist to drop off a load when these plants aren't included.

For moisture retention, for appearance, and for avoiding muddy shoes, a much thinner layer of mulch will do. For a chaparral garden, where inorganic (say, gravel) mulch or shredded bark is used, a few inches go a long way. Deeper bark or wood mulches can promote undesirable fungal growth when combined with moisture. This is a particular problem if the mulch is fine instead of chunky. Judiciously augment the mulch around—but not on—your new plants. Just as a good covering of mulch suppresses weeds, it also subdues native annuals. So while mulching around your wildflower seedlings is fine, be careful not to cover them. In all gardens, keep the mulch away from stems and trunks.

Water

If the month is dry, extend the natural range of winter rainfall to keep your plants growing while it's still relatively cool. Keep in mind that the

These buckwheat seedlings can be planted now, but they'll need regular water until their roots develop.
HELEN POPPER

plants that will go without summer water are the ones that will make the most of the water that they get now. If rain is absent this month, consider watering the summer-dry corners of your garden, soaking the area deeply as our rains might do.

WHAT'S IN BLOOM?

Early spring brings the bright orange blooms of the bush monkeyflower (*Mimulus aurantiacus, M. longiflorus*) to the Transverse Range. An adaptable, short-lived perennial, the bush monkeyflower is often used in revegetation projects. It is a larval host to the common checkerspot butterfly and it provides nectar to bees and hummingbirds. On the same slopes, blue

In the shade of an oak, a hound's tongue blooms.
JUDY KRAMER

Frying pans (*Eschscholzia lobbii*) brighten a garden meadow. HELEN POPPER

dicks (*Dichelostemma capitatum,* also called wild hyacinth) bloom on single stems above grass-like leaves. The flowers provide nectar for butterflies, and the plants naturalize easily.

Near the Delta, blue flowers grace the arching stems of hound's tongue (*Cynoglossum grande*) under an oak. Swaths of bright yellow Johnny jump-ups (*Viola pedunculata*) and of baby blue-eyes (*Nemophila menziesii*) stretch out along the edge of the tree's canopy. A ring of California poppies (*Eschscholzia californica*) and early penstemons (*Penstemon* spp.) frames the scene. The hound's tongue returns larger each year from deep roots, and the baby blue-eyes self-sow. Big patches of Johnny jump-ups have an added attraction when they are planted in semi-rural areas around

San Francisco Bay: they host the endangered callippe silverspot butterfly. Callippe silverspots lay their eggs on the spent foliage, and their larvae nibble the plants when they resprout the following year.

In the diminutive sunny border of a Central Coast garden, the deep yellow of California buttercup (*Ranunculus californicus*) combines with the cool hues of dog violet (*Viola adunca*) and blue-eyed grass (*Sisyrinchium bellum*). Stepping into nearby dappled shade, we find neat mounds of delicate foliage. There, on long stems, rise the bright red and yellow flowers of western columbine (*Aquilegia formosa*) and the pink-white panicles of shaggy alumroot (*Heuchera pilosissima*). Farther back under denser cover sit the luminous white blooms of western wakerobin (*Trillium ovatum*). Each large, smooth flower floats on a hidden stem above a triad of broad leaves. The enchanting blooms seem to call us from the still, deep shade.

Flowers

April

Tranquil violets (*Viola* spp.) dot the redwood forest floor. Ephemeral fairy rings of downingia (*Downingia* spp.) surround vernal pools. Goldfields (*Lasthenia californica*), tidy-tips (*Layia platyglossa*), cream cups (*Platystemon californicus*), and lupines (*Lupinus* spp.) sweep across the state's grasslands. It is mid-spring, and California is alive with flowers.

The bounty of blooms is captured in our native gardens. Annual wildflowers burst forth, self-sown in some gardens, carefully hand-sown and tended in others. The annuals join bulbs, perennials, and shrubs in an overlapping cascade of color.

Take it all in. Pick a posy. Pinch back a few blooms here, a little new growth there. Take a few cuttings from roots and stems. Sow the seeds of a few more annuals if you like, then

◀ Iris and wildflowers decorate a fescue meadow at Strybing Arboretum in San Francisco.
SAXON HOLT

APRIL'S JOBS

Plant and sow

Plant riparian and redwood understory plants—anything that will continue to get water. Sow the seeds of warm-season grasses.

Do—and don't—water

Do keep watering all new plantings, especially seedlings, as the rain abates. Don't water spent bulbs. Don't water areas that don't need it: dryness is your ally in weed abatement.

Mulch

Mulch helps retain moisture, so add it where needed before we move into the dry season. It is not needed near trunks of trees and shrubs or the crowns of perennials, where it can promote fungal disease.

Prune, just a little

Pinch back flowering shrubs as their blooms fade. Clean out deadwood. If the rains have largely passed, then thin shrubs and trees if genuinely needed.

Take cuttings

Give root cuttings a try with Oregon grape (*Berberis aquifolium*) or kinnikinnick (*Arctostaphylos uva-ursi*). Take stem cuttings of wax myrtle (*Myrica californica*) or white sage (*Salvia apiana*).

Keep aphids in check

Look for aphids on fast-growing plants, especially on the underside of leaves. Hose them off while the colonies are still small.

Manage weeds

Keep bare, disturbed ground to a minimum. Dig up ivy (*Hedera helix*) and Himalayan blackberry (*Rubus discolor*). Pull up warm-season annual weeds while they are still small.

Celebrate Earth Day

Enjoy your garden, tend it, and share its bounty. Share cuttings with friends and nectar with hummingbirds. Enjoy other gardens too: take a native garden tour or visit a botanic garden.

carefully water them in. Water is key. Plant anything you will water, and water anything that you have planted. Along the way, keep a keen eye out for weeds, and keep a keener eye out for beauty to enjoy.

NATIVE GARDENING IN APRIL
Plant and Sow

If your garden—or a corner of it—will have moisture over the coming months, then you can continue a spring-fever planting spree. Set out plants that you would find near creeks, seeps, and the foggy coast. For example, creek dogwood (*Cornus sericea*), western spicebush (*Calycanthus occidentalis*), twinberry (*Lonicera involucrata*), and red elderberry (*Sambucus racemosa*) will all do well if set out now. These grow best planted in or near a watered area, such as a lawn, or in moist locales that mimic the conditions where these plants originate.

You can still sow annual wildflower seeds now if you will have the patience to water them. Most spring-sown annuals will be smaller than those sown in fall, with correspondingly smaller flowers or shorter bloom periods, but they still will add beauty to the garden. After removing any weedy competition, sow them and water them in—very gently. Avoid forming a torrent with your hose, which will wash away small seeds and knock down young seedlings. If you are looking for perennial cover from seed, you can follow the same weed-sow-water routine with yarrow (*Achillea millefolium*). Yarrow is easy to grow, and with minimal water it provides a cover of vibrant, ferny foliage and long-lasting blooms.

This is a good time to sow warm-season grasses. While most of our native grasses are cool-season ones, which should be sown or planted in fall, there is still a nice assortment of warm-season grasses available for sowing now. These range from the diminutive to the architectural. Blue grama (*Bouteloua gracilis*) grows just a few inches tall, with spikes about a foot high. It slowly forms a sod. Alkali sacaton (*Sporobolus airoides*) and deer grass (*Muhlenbergia rigens*) are rugged and large, with plumes reaching as high as five feet. In between in stature are Diego bentgrass (*Agrostis pallens,* which can be grown as a warm- or cool-season grass) and purple threeawn (*Aristida purpurea*). Diego bentgrass reaches one or two feet high, but it can be mowed—perhaps monthly or so—watered (with good drainage), and used as a dense turf. Field sedge (*Carex praegracilis*) is quite like a grass and is also used as a lawn replacement where there is more moisture. Purple threeawn also grows to a foot or two, but it is ideal when left in its narrow, iconic vertical clumps. Like the sowing of seeds for annuals, the sowing of grass seeds first requires thorough removal of weeds, then follow-up water.

If you already have mature Diego bentgrass or blue grama, you can divide it now. You also can divide clustered field sedge. Compared to seeding, propagation from division gives grasses and grass-like plants a head start over the weeds. Division of some of the other warm-season grasses is difficult. Some of the toughest growers, such as deer grass and alkali sacaton, are also the toughest to divide.

Taper off planting anything that will require summer dormancy or drought, such as flannel bush (*Fremontodendron californicum*), hound's tongue (*Cynoglossum grande*), and scarlet larkspur (*Delphinium cardinale*). Wait until fall before you let them tempt you.

Do—and Don't—Water

If it doesn't rain, then water young plants, especially the young seedlings from your March sowing. Do not forget your young drought-tolerant plants. Even dry-garden plants need regular water to get established. Deep watering is best, and as the plants become larger, the frequency should be decreased.

Water native bulbs—including those that require summer drought—as long as they are green or have not yet bloomed. You can also feed native bulbs now, if they are growing in pots. Feed them a small amount of bone meal or a very weak balanced fertilizer. You can continue watering the bulbs right up until the time that they begin to collapse. In some areas, shooting stars (*Dodecatheon* spp.) are already collapsing, signaling you to back off with the water and let them rest.

If drought-tolerant plants are well established in the summer-dry areas of your garden, you have a choice about water. You can water now, extending spring and giving the plants something in the bank for later. Or you can back off watering these areas now, even if it does not rain.

Knowing that dormancy may arrive a bit earlier this way, you also know that you're saving yourself some water and the trouble of future weeds.

Mulch

Mulch is important in getting a new native garden started. Add a layer now to retain moisture in the coming dry season, and to help suppress weeds. By improving soil structure over time, mulching now can even make fall planting easier. (For information on mulching materials, see the discussion in February, pages 69–73.)

Prune, Just a Little

Take a retiring approach to pruning this month. As you walk around the garden and see a few fading blooms on ceanothus (*Ceanothus* spp.), manzanita (*Arctostaphylos* spp.), and other spring-flowering shrubs, you might pinch back the stems a bit. This follows up on the pinching you

Remove deadwood tangled in pipestem clematis, so its flowers can be appreciated.
PAUL FURMAN

may have done in March, on those plants that send out new growth on the ends of their branches, past their flowers. If the deer don't continue "pinching" for you, doing it yourself will help keep those plants filled in.

April is also a good time to remove any leftover deadwood that is tangled in perennials and shrubs, such as Pacific aster (*Aster chilensis*), virgin's bower (*Clematis ligusticifolia*), various ferns, sage (*Salvia* spp.), and toyon (*Heteromeles arbutifolia*). In those areas where the rains have passed, you may begin to gently shape young plants, perhaps thinning just a little to let light reach the lower branches. Use a delicate hand. This is not a time to eliminate spring growth and the cover it provides for nesting birds. Instead, it is a time to clean it up, occasionally to direct it, and always to appreciate it.

Take Cuttings

Many shrubs and perennials can be successfully propagated from cuttings now. Cuttings taken from roots are usually easy to grow; cuttings from stems require a bit more care. The latter need regular misting to avoid drying out. Nurseries often use greenhouses, with misters that are on timers, and they provide bottom heat for both root and stem cuttings. They make sure their rooting medium is sterile, and they use various combinations of peat (not for sages, it stays too wet), perlite, vermiculite, or coarse sand. Home gardeners more often make do with a kitchen counter and a greenhouse that is sometimes nothing more than a loosely propped clear plastic bag or a gallon milk container with the bottom cut off. A rooting medium may be as uncomplicated as coarse sand in a container with good drainage. Ever practical, home gardeners trade off the likelihood of some losses for the opportunity to experiment with propagation.

Give root cuttings a try now using the rhizomes of upright or creeping Oregon grape (*Berberis aquifolium* var. *aquifolium* or *B. aquifolium* var. *repens*), or using the rooted stems of kinnikinnick (*Arctostaphylos uva-ursi*). To take the cuttings, unearth a bit of the roots with a trowel or shovel, and choose vigorous lengths of root that are roughly the thickness of a pencil. Cut segments about six inches long. Keeping the cuttings moist, position them in the rooting medium with the same side up as you found them. They

An improvised "greenhouse" keeps cuttings moist. HELEN POPPER

are likely to need to stay in the medium for a month or more. You will know they are ready for potting up in soil when new green growth shows itself.

Try stem cuttings of ceanothus (*Ceanothus* spp.) that have bloomed, of wax myrtle (*Myrica californica*), and of perennials, such as California mountain fuchsia (*Epilobium canum*), California aster (*Lessingia filaginifolia*), white sage (*Salvia apiana*), or Cleveland sage (*S. clevelandii*). For pinemat manzanita (*Arctostaphylos nevadensis*), take a cutting of a few inches of year-old woody growth. For ceanothus, wax myrtle, and sage, take cuttings of roughly six inches from the soft new growth at the ends of the branches. (For more on stem cuttings, see the discussion in November, pages 35–37.)

Water and mist your cuttings regularly, but don't overdo it—especially for the sages, which are prone to rotting. Rooting hormone improves the odds for all but the fuchsia.

New wax myrtle roots are especially brittle, so take extra care when you lift the cuttings out of the rooting medium and pot them up into containers. The stem cuttings are ready to move to pots at the first sign of new growth, but be prepared to wait two to three months before you see any on the stem cuttings of shrubs.

Keep Aphids in Check

Aphids thrive in gardens that are rich in nitrogen, so they tend to be less of a problem in native gardens than in conventional ones. However, they still can be annoying on the new spring growth of many perennials, such as buckwheat (*Eriogonum* spp.), bitter root (*Lewisia rediviva*), mallow (*Malacothamnus* spp.), penstemon (*Penstemon* spp.), and sage (*Salvia* spp.); on some shrubs, including ceanothus (*Ceanothus* spp.) and toyon (*Heteromeles arbutifolia*); and on some young trees, such as California bay laurel (*Umbellularia californica*).

Take a close look at the new growth in your garden. Pay special attention to the underside of leaves, where aphids seem to congregate, and to the upwind side of your garden, where they may first arrive from neighboring areas. If you find mainly mummified aphids, then you can relax: it means that parasitic wasps are catching up with the aphids. Harmless to us, the wasps will take care of the major infestations for you. If instead you find colonies of live aphids, hose them off with jets of water. You may have to repeat the spraying every few days.

If you notice a trail of ants making its way up the trunk of a tree or shrub, it's likely that the ants are tending and protecting aphids. In that case, you may want to control the aphids by controlling the ants. One approach is to wrap a band of sticky material around the plant's trunk, near the base, to stop the ants. If you choose to use a chemical control, use a slow-acting selective control in a bait station. Bait stations prevent the poison from evaporating, and they offer some pet resistance. Their slow action allows foraging ants to bring the poison back to weaken the entire nest. Their selectivity means that they won't harm the parasitic wasps or other natural predators of the aphids.

Manage Weeds

Weeding is an ongoing job in any garden, native or not, and April brings weeds to us all. Cool-season annual weeds still bedevil us, while warm-season ones are already popping up. Native gardeners can take heart from the fact that the need for weeding will abate as the native garden matures.

For native gardens carved out of a lawn or a long-untended plot, a predictable pattern of weed management follows the garden's development. For these gardens, the first step is to clear away the lawn or weeds— perhaps a bramble of blackberry (*Rubus discolor*), a hillside of pampas grass or jubata grass (*Cortaderia selloana* or *C. jubata*), a parking strip of ivy (*Hedera helix*), or a patch of Bermuda grass (*Cynodon dactylon*). However large or small the initial area, clearing it is a big, often satisfying step.

Lamentably, the satisfaction wanes with the realization that what now replaces the weeds is a weed magnet: bare, disturbed soil. If left this way in mid-spring, the plot invites warm-season annual weeds or worse: invasive woody perennials, such as French or Scotch broom, that may sprout from seeds left long ago. Timely action to make the newly bared earth inhospitable to weeds is the only sure road back to contentment. Cover the disturbed soil with a deep layer of mulch, or sow and plant native garden pioneers that can vanquish the weeds. Garden pioneers might include robust annuals, fast-growing shrubs, such as coyote bush (*Baccharis pilularis*) in sunny spots near the coast or creek dogwood

(*Cornus sericea*) in wet or poorly drained sites, or even trees, such as white alder (*Alnus rhombifolia*) and Fremont cottonwood (*Populus fremontii*) in wet areas. These still can be planted now as long as they will have water—until fall rains come for the coyote bush, and year-round for the rest. Once mulch and pioneer plants are in place, competition from weeds can be managed. There will always be fresh weedy incursions, but they will be easier to suppress.

In the garden's next phase, slower-growing natives establish themselves, replacing the mulch and some of the pioneer plants. From time to time, some leftover weeds, such as English ivy (*Hedera helix*) or Himalayan blackberry (*Rubus discolor*), will reemerge. Dig them out if you can, perhaps with an enthusiastic, gloved little helper on spring break from school. As the succeeding native plantings mature, they drop their own mulch, alter the soil, and shade out competition. Weeds become less vigorous, and experience makes them easier to spot early on. In addition, many weeds that trouble conventional gardens (plantain, sedges, and spurge) do not trouble established summer-dry native gardens simply because they lack adequate water. The mature natives themselves become an increasingly reliable part of your weed-fighting arsenal.

Celebrate Earth Day

You are the steward of your garden. Enjoy it. Open the window, feel the air, listen to a towhee, smell a sage, watch a bumblebee. Step outside and walk lazily to a corner—or to every corner—of your garden. If you are so inclined, pull a bit of mulch away from the base of a shrub, pinch a few of its tips, nab a weed, or pick a posy along the way. The plants, their inhabitants, and the spaces between them comprise the ever-changing media of your Earth Day canvas.

You may want to peruse and enjoy others' gardens too. In mid-spring, California's native plant enthusiasts routinely swing open their garden gates for visitors. If you are in the San Francisco area, register for the Bringing Back the Natives tours in the East Bay or the Going Natives Garden Tour on the Peninsula and in the South Bay; or just show up in the city itself for the Native Plant Garden Tour of the California Native Plant Society's Yerba Buena chapter. Farther north, local chapters of the

Guests on a native garden tour enjoy flannel bush atop a knoll and lupine, alumroot, iris, and poppy on a Berkeley hillside. This particular garden was started in the 1950s by two of the founders of the California Native Plant Society. HELEN POPPER

society offer tours in Redding and El Dorado. In Los Angeles, you can sign up for the self-guided Theodore Payne Native Plant Garden Tour, or reserve a spot on the guided Spring Garden Tour organized by the South Coast chapter of the California Native Plant Society. In Orange County, take the Native Garden Tour organized by the Native Plant Society's local chapter. The number and quality of native garden tours just keeps rising.

At any of these, you might be lured into a companion event: a plant sale, a flower show, a lecture, a class, or a hike. Whether you wind up in your own garden, in another's, in a classroom, or in the wilderness, celebrate the spirit of Earth Day.

WHAT'S IN BLOOM?

There's a good reason that many native garden tours are scheduled in April. As John Steinbeck wrote in 1932 in *The Pastures of Heaven*, "It was the loveliest season of the year; lupins and shooting stars, gallitos and wild violets smoldered with color in the new, short grass on the hillsides. The oaks had put on new leaves as shiny and clean as washed holly." That loveliness is with us still. Feeding on the rains of winter, growing in the warmth of early spring, our natives deliver their show, and the state explodes with color.

Annual wildflowers paint the grasslands gold, purple, blue, and white.

Baby blue-eyes, tidy-tips, and goldfields bloom at Shell Creek in San Luis Obispo County. JUDY KRAMER

With little or no supplemental water, native iris blooms reliably each spring. HELEN POPPER

Goldfields (*Lasthenia californica*), tidy-tips (*Layia platyglossa*), purple owl's clover (*Castilleja exserta*), gilias (*Gilia* spp.), lupines (*Lupinus* spp.), and cream cups (*Platystemon californicus*) blanket the fields in places like Antelope Valley, Bear Valley, the Carrizo Plain, and North Table Mountain.

Colors cascade down the slopes and into the meadows of the Peninsular and Transverse Ranges. There, too, the purple and blues of owl's clover and lupines set off goldfields and cream cups. On the Santa Rosa Plateau, checkerbloom (*Sidalcea malvaeflora*) and fairy lanterns (*Calochortus albus*) bloom alongside fields of shooting stars (*Dodecatheon clevelandii*), blue dicks (*Dichelostemma capitatum*), and California buttercups (*Ranunculus californicus*).

To these beauties, coastal communities add the drama of red larkspur (*Delphinium nudicaule*) and red maids (*Calandrinia ciliata*), the blue of western dog violets (*Viola adunca*), and a palette of Indian paintbrushes (*Castilleja* spp., cousins of purple owl's clover).

In the deep shade of the coast redwoods in the north, few annuals make such lavish displays, but many perennials bloom delightfully now. Redwood sorrels (*Oxalis oregana*) show their pretty faces, along with bleeding hearts (*Dicentra formosa*), stream and redwood violets (*Viola glabella* and *V. sempervirens*), and fairybells (*Prosartes hookeri* and *P. smithii*).

Gardens throughout the state echo these sights and create them anew. Blue dicks (*Dichelostemma capitatum*) combine with bitter root (*Lewisia rediviva*) in a garden wall. Violets (*Viola* spp.) peek out from under western azaleas (*Rhododendron occidentale*). Goldfields (*Lasthenia californica*), lupines (*Lupinus* sp.), and gilias (*Gilia* spp.) show off in beds, in drifts between shrubs on newly planted hillsides, and tucked between bunchgrasses in a garden meadow. Checkerblooms (*Sidalcea malvaeflora*) and seep monkeyflowers (*Mimulus guttatus*) punctuate the edges of ponds. Native gardens resound with spring.

Collect Your Seeds

May

It is Act II of the spring garden show: exit riotous annual wildflowers, enter perennial blooms. Our garden tasks echo the progression. Now is the time to let annual wildflowers set seed. It is the time to appreciate the bold opening salvos of penstemons, sages, monkeyflowers, and buckwheats, and it is time to deadhead them for continued blooms through the end of spring and into summer.

May is also a month to water if you choose: water to coax a little more bloom from annuals, water on the coast if it has been windy, water anywhere you like if it has been unusually dry. Outside of California's northwest corner, this is the last month before the onset of the natural summer drought that shapes so many of our gardens. The soil is still relatively cool. When it warms up in summer, those of us with chaparral gardens will withhold water to avoid the fatal

❮ Grape soda lupine grows in the photographer's garden. STEPHEN INGRAM

Let wildflower seeds ripen

Let some of your annuals set seed. The ripening seeds will draw foraging birds to your garden, and you can collect some for next year's fall planting.

Pinch and prune

Selectively pinch and prune for repeat blooms and shrubs that are healthy and attractive.

Propagate with cuttings

This is a good time to take cuttings of shrubs and a few perennials. Among the easiest this month are snowberry (*Symphoricarpos albus*) and yerba buena (*Satureja douglasii*).

Water now, before the heat of summer

To extend the growing period, you can water most plants (but not spent bulbs) as long as it is not too hot. Water deeply, then let the area dry out for a time before watering again.

Plant and sow

Plant riparian and coastal plants that will continue to receive moisture through the summer. Sow another round of annual wildflower seeds if you plan to water them.

Weed and mulch

Pull out warm-season weeds as they come up. Keep them at bay with mulch. Spread the mulch thickly, but as always, keep it away from the root crowns of trees and shrubs; the plants will need good air circulation come summer. Where invasive annual grasses have come in too thickly to weed them, mow them down now, before they set seed.

fungi of warm, moist soil. For now, in the mildness of May, we can still water judiciously to fill out spring.

NATIVE GARDENING IN MAY
Let Wildflower Seeds Ripen—for Birds and for You

As you begin to tidy up your garden this month, pause before simply pulling out spent annuals from your wildflower beds. Consider leaving some of the faded beauties in place, letting them go to seed. When left briefly in place, many wildflowers readily self-sow. Their natural reproduction saves work and expense the following year. Clarkias (*Clarkia* spp.) and California poppies (*Eschscholzia californica*) reseed with abandon. Baby blue-eyes (*Nemophila menziesii*), tidy-tips (*Layia platyglossa*), and gilias (especially globe gilia, *Gilia capitata*, and bird's-eye gilia, *G. tricolor*) also return each year when given the chance to set their seeds.

Ripe seeds bring into the garden the added delight of foraging birds. While all our wildflowers will draw in the seed-eaters, some birds seem to specialize. California quail are particularly fond of legumes, such as lupines (*Lupinus* spp.) and native clovers (*Trifolium* spp.). Mourning doves favor the seeds of red maids (*Calandrinia ciliata*) and California poppies

Tidy-tips readily self-sow.

JUDY KRAMER

113

(*Eschscholzia californica*). The fading flowers need not stay in place long to provide a bounty for the birds: the seeds of annuals typically mature just a few weeks after their peak bloom.

If the annuals grow in formal beds, where their seed heads and faded foliage seem out of place, you can still provide for the birds. Simply pull the faded annuals, seed heads and all, and lay or scatter them in a more casual or less used corner of the garden. Some of the seeds will continue to ripen, and the foraging birds will find them. If the corner lies behind tangled thickets or dense, thorny shrubs, so much the better. The close cover provides a refuge from predators, such as house cats and raptors.

COLLECT SEEDS You may want to gather, dry, and store some of your annual seeds for planting in fall or for sharing with friends. Most seeds are best collected when they are ripe—when they rattle in their capsules, or when the capsules dry, change color, or fall easily from the plant. After collecting the seed capsules, let them continue to dry out in a paper bag or a loosely covered container that allows air to circulate. Check the bag or container for insects from time to time. A few seeds, including poppy and lupine seeds, burst forth from the capsules when they ripen. (That is, they dehisce.) So you must either collect them just a little bit early or secure small paper bags around the seed capsules while the capsules are still on the plant. Either approach will enable you to capture the seeds before the pods pop open and disperse them.

When the seeds are completely dry, separate them from the rest of the plant material. You will find that some seeds need to be crushed between your fingers or under a rolling pin to be separated. Others need only to be shaken through a sieve or onto the bottom of a shallow bowl. Shaking will separate the seeds from the chaff, which can be gently blown away with a puff of breath or a light breeze. Put the clean, dry seeds into paper envelopes or small paper bags. Store them somewhere cool, dry, and dark but not airtight. Experienced gardeners label the seed packets with the plant's type, the date taken, and any special characteristics that might otherwise be forgotten. Fall is a long way away.

Pinch and Prune

Bring spring within bounds and prepare for summer with some selective pinching and pruning. You will be rewarded with renewed blooms, with perennials and shrubs that can support their profuse blooms, and with more balanced growth.

Where you are not letting seeds ripen, cut back annuals and biennials that have finished their first wave of bloom. Deadhead penstemon (*Penstemon* spp.) and remove the spent or rangy flower stocks of bush monkeyflower (*Mimulus aurantiacus*) for mid-summer flowers. Pinch back long stems of the tall varieties of California fuchsia (*Epilobium* spp.) so the stems will be able to support profuse blooms later. (The low-growing varieties need only the annual or biennial light shearing of winter.)

If you have not already cleaned up island morning glory (*Calystegia macrostegia*) or deer grass (*Muhlenbergia rigens*), prune them if they are looking rough. Clean out the dead material first; only then should you take the clippers to the live material. For the morning glory, choose the stems you want to keep. If you keep everything, the lower portion of this fast-growing vine will be shaded and become bare over the years.

Many shrubs benefit from some pinching after they have flowered. Without pinching, the new growth of ceanothus (*Ceanothus* spp.) and manzanita (*Arctostaphylos* spp.) may begin beyond the spent flowers, leaving bare branches behind. Pinching just one-quarter inch behind the spent blooms is enough, whether for large shrubs or ground-hugging forms. For denser growth, tree anemone (*Carpenteria californica,* also called bush anemone), chamise (*Adenostoma fasciculatum*), and Nevin's barberry (*Berberis nevinii*) may all be pinched after flowering.

Clean out any deadwood from mountain mahogany (*Cercocarpus betuloides*) and inspect it to see if it will benefit from the removal of suckers or crossing branches. Selective pruning will open up the shrub and reveal its pretty bark. Remove a few old stems of Oregon grape (*Berberis* spp.). Cutting them nearly to the ground allows for fuller growth in the remainder of the shrub. Lightly prune holly-leaf cherry (*Prunus ilicifolia*) after flowering, and—if needed—prune wax myrtle (*Myrica californica*) now, before the summer heat.

Propagate with Cuttings

May is a good month to take cuttings of several shrubs and perennials. Among deciduous shrubs, try taking cuttings of golden currant (*Ribes aureum*), wild mock orange (*Philadelphus lewisii*), or snowberry (*Symphoricarpos albus*). Golden currant volunteers in southern California from the seeds that birds drop, it spreads easily through layering, and it can be propagated from cuttings in late spring. (For more on layering, see the discussion in February, pages 75–76. For treatment of hardwood and softwood cuttings, see November, pages 35–37.) If a friend has a particularly nice one, ask to take cuttings when the stems firm up a bit, and use a mild rooting hormone. To share a mock orange, the sweet northern California bloomer, take cuttings from the tips of the leafy thin stems of its side branches. With hormone, they will root in about a month and be ready to plant in fall. Snowberry is the easiest of the three to root from cuttings. Like the golden currant, it also can be propagated by layering. Taken now, snowberry's softwood cuttings usually will form roots with or without hormone. They, too, will be ready for planting in a hospitable location in fall.

Among evergreen shrubs, coyote bush (*Baccharis pilularis*) takes well from cuttings now. Coyote bush is regularly grown from cuttings because the male and female plants play different roles in the garden, and most gardeners strongly prefer one sex over the other. Gardeners who want a well-groomed evergreen shrub choose the male plant. With its small leaves and inconspicuous flowers, the male is reminiscent of boxwood, though with its own spicy scent. The females, in contrast, carry masses of puffy seed heads that some gardeners find objectionable. Gardeners of a different stripe admire the seed heads and the sparrows they attract. Lester Rowntree, author of *Flowering Shrubs of California,* wrote fondly in 1939 of the seed head's "airy white fleece." Whatever your choice, softwood cuttings taken now and treated with rooting hormone have a good chance of success.

May often is also the best month to take tree anemone (*Carpenteria californica*) cuttings, though they are not as easy to root because the cuttings often wilt. However, the shrub benefits from a bit of pruning after it flowers. If you do prune this month, you will have some stems to work with, and it is natural to give cuttings a try. They will root best if you use the supple but firm tips. Use only the mildest rooting hormone, and take care not to break the delicate roots when you pot them up.

Cuttings of some perennials, such as California goldenrod (*Solidago californica*) and yerba buena (*Satureja douglasii*), also can be taken. By May, goldenrods have emerged from dormancy and grown a bit, but they have not flowered. Take cuttings from stems that, while still succulent, have firmed up. Yerba buena grows horizontally, so it makes sense to lay the

This yerba buena is ready to propagate from cuttings. It mingles here with (nonnative) thyme. HELEN POPPER

117

cuttings that way in the rooting medium. Bury the nodes about one-half inch deep, letting the tiny leaves protrude. Four-inch cuttings should be long enough. Most will develop roots and can be potted up in about four weeks.

Water Now, Before the Heat of Summer

Coastal gardens will need extra water if the wind has been strong. Inland gardens may need water in preparation for summer. If it has been a dry season or a dry month, provide some extra water to everything in your garden except bulbs: withhold water when they finish flowering.

The soil is still relatively cool this month. As soon as the soil warms up (usually in June), it will be time to cut back on water for many of our natives. This is especially true of chaparral plants, which can suffer from the fungal pathogens that proliferate in warm, moist soil. A few deep waterings now—perhaps every two weeks—will put your garden in good stead before the rigors of summer.

Plant and Sow

Plants from riparian and redwood communities can be put in the ground now as long as they will receive the summer moisture they require. Oddly enough, this is also a good time to plant some desert plants, such as the California fan palm (*Washingtonia filifera*). While we rightly think of fan palms as desert plants, our oasis images make sense too. Their presence in the wild indicates a water source, such as a seep or stream. They grow in summer, and they can be planted now.

If your garden is a riparian one or near the coast, then you can continue to sow annual wildflower seeds for summer blooms (though they may not be quite as dazzling as spring's). With regular moisture, you will be able to coax summer blooms from clarkias (*Clarkia* spp.), poppies (*Eschscholzia californica*), sunflowers (*Helianthus annuus*), Chinese houses (*Collinsia heterophylla*), and California bluebells (*Phacelia campanularia*, also called desert bluebells), as well as bee-friendly tansy-leaf phacelia (*P. tanacetifolia*). You can also broadcast the seeds of deer grass (*Muhlenbergia rigens*) now or in early summer.

Warm-season weeds begin to grow in earnest this month. Pull them now, before they mature and before the soil hardens. Pull crabgrass (*Digitaria* spp.), knotweed (*Polygonum arenastrum*), kikuyugrass (*Pennisetum clandestinum*), and spotted spurge (*Euphorbia maculata*, an ant magnet). Thoroughly dig out young bindweed (*Convolvulus arvensis*) and Bermuda grass (*Cynodon dactylon*) as soon as they appear. If you have an area of invasive exotic grass that is too large to remove, mow it back now, before it sets seeds. This is particularly important in areas where fire is a real risk.

Keep weeds at bay by mulching heavily over much of the garden's open soil, but leave a few bare areas—perhaps in the dry areas of the garden, or under shrubs—for our shy native bees to nest in. As always, keep mulch away from the root crowns of trees and shrubs so that it won't trap moisture there.

WHAT'S IN BLOOM?

The exuberant blooms of California's native perennials take center stage in May. With bold colors and abundant displays, their flowers grab the attention of people and pollinators alike.

Spires of scarlet larkspur (*Delphinium cardinale*) draw hummingbirds to a summer-dry garden on a sunny bluff. The flower stalks reach up to six feet high, and hummingbirds dart easily from them to the tall lavender-blue columns of royal penstemon (*Penstemon spectabilis*). Like most (but not all) native pestemon, royal penstemon requires dry summers. Its smaller cousin, foothill penstemon (*P. heterophyllus*), can tolerate some summer water. Penstemon provides native gardeners with a rich palette of blues, purples, pinks, and even creamy whites.

Butterflies feed nearby in the sun on mounds of flowering buckwheat. California, coast, cliff, and sulfur buckwheat (*Eriogonum fasciculatum, E. latifolium, E. parvifolium,* and *E. umbellatum*) typically begin their long blooming season now. Sage (*Salvia* spp.), woolly sunflower (*Eriophyllum lanatum*), California phacelia (*Phacelia californica*), and cow parsnip (*Heracleum lanatum*) help fill out the butterflies' spring banquet.

Butterflies share the buckwheat with bumblebees—the fuzzy gentle giants of the bee world. Bumblebees also favor penstemon and sage, along with the blue pea-like flowers of silver bush lupine (*Lupinus albifrons*) and grape soda lupine (*L. excubitus*). These lupines open their spires of blooms week after week in billowy blue masses.

Hummingbirds are equally well fed in a garden with some high shade and a bit of moisture. There they can enjoy scarlet monkeyflower

(*Mimulus cardinalis*), coral bells (*Heuchera* spp.), Indian pink (*Silene californica*), leopard lily (*Lilium pardalinum*), and wood mint (*Stachys bullata*, also called hedge nettle, although it does not sting). They share western columbine (*Aquilegia formosa*) and the last blooms of hummingbird sage (*Salvia spathacea*) with the butterflies.

Professional garden designers often suggest that small plants be grouped together to make an arresting visual impact. It is not just people who appreciate such arrangements. Pollinators, including hummingbirds, butterflies, and bees, all take notice of groupings of a single species when looking for a hospitable place to alight. Tempt them into the garden with a bed or two of solid color in May. Once there, they will discover the other flowering plants that will sustain them.

June

Foggy coastal air pushes against the elemental blue of inland skies. A moving wall between them keeps one side cool and the other hot. On the cool side, little water is needed, and little is given. On the hot side, plants might be thirsty, but too much water will damage them, and nature withholds it. From now until fall, most of the state will receive no rain.

In our gardens, we might echo nature's drought but not follow it slavishly. Even many established gardens benefit from one deep soak in June, as long as the weather is not too hot. Young plants will need more frequent soaks, though for most, the soil should dry out between waterings.

Without water, most weeds slow their growth, and our garden chores slow with them. We might fix irrigation systems, take a few cuttings, and plant some warm-season grasses. Mostly, though, we can enjoy the garden as it transitions

◀ Tree anemones provide subtly scented, old-fashioned blooms. STEPHEN INGRAM

JUNE'S JOBS

Water wisely

Water deeply enough to thoroughly soak the soil, but water infrequently enough to allow it to dry out before you water again. Avoid watering during heat waves: the combination of heat and moisture promotes root rot and crown rot in many natives.

Check, repair, and adjust irrigation

Try out your watering system. Look for pooling and dry areas. As plants mature, move the source of water farther from their centers.

Clean up shrubs, groundcovers, and perennials

Deadhead perennials and remove deadwood from shrubs. Edge low-growing manzanitas (*Arctostaphylos* spp.). Selectively prune chamise (*Adenostoma fasciculatum*), redshanks (*A. sparsifolium*), Oregon grape (*Berberis* spp.), and large manzanitas.

Take cuttings

Propagate from cuttings of shrubs and trees, such as red elderberry (*Sambucus racemosa*), toyon (*Heteromeles arbutifolia*), big-leaf maple (*Acer macrophyllum*), and creek dogwood (*Cornus sericea*). Many will be ready to plant out in fall.

Solarize a lawn

To replace a lawn, you need to kill it first. Covering it with clear plastic for a month will do the trick inland, where the long days of June heat things up.

Plant and sow where there is water

Where you will water, you can set out warm-season grasses and redwood and riparian plants. Where there is some protection from the most intense summer heat, you also can sow more wildflower seeds.

from spring's bright delights to summer's own distinctive blooms and textures. Children may race out of the last day of school, but we can relax in the long evenings, knowing the garden's slow season is ahead of us.

NATIVE GARDENING IN JUNE
Water Wisely

IN THE WILD While there is always some moisture near redwoods and waterways, California will get little or no actual rainfall from now until October. Most of the state's natives evolved with this summer drought. Knowing this, we might be tempted to just forget about water all summer long. However, close observation of plants in the wild tells us that our native gardens may suffer if we skip summer watering altogether. Most natives—even chaparral plants—benefit from some summer moisture, especially when they are young.

Consider the fate of the seedlings of our familiar toyon (*Heteromeles arbutifolia*). Birds disperse them in the wild, and plenty of seedlings take root, yet few survive except in unusually wet years. We find the lucky ones nestled in the deep litter of a very old stand of chaparral, protected by the shade of its canopy.

Most gardens are not so hospitable to young plants. We (quite sensibly) site new plants to satisfy their needs once they mature. Unlike birds, we plant them singly or in small numbers. We plant them far enough from one another to give them room to grow to maturity. We often plant toyon in the sun and in well-drained soil, where moisture dissipates quickly. The roots of seedlings and of plants fresh from containers—regardless of the container size—are small and undeveloped. With their immature root systems, young plants cannot survive most garden conditions in summer without added water.

Many established plants also benefit from supplemental water. While most species survive drought in their own habitats, some make it only by going dormant early in the summer. In excessively dry years, many plants simply die. Nature makes up for the losses through renewed growth and the success of new seedlings in wet years. If we emulate nature's summer drought in our gardens, we must resign ourselves to emulating its recurring plant losses in the driest years and to long summer dormancy. By watering just a few times during summer—but not too much and certainly not too often—we can keep our gardens healthy and attractive.

HOW MUCH WATER? There are two rules of thumb for watering California's native gardens in summer. The first rule of thumb is to water deeply, so that the water penetrates the surrounding soil well beyond the reach of the roots. That means watering slowly so that lots of water will soak in, rather than run off. While you can go ahead and hose the plants off too—to keep them looking nice—the important thing is to soak the soil around them. The second rule of thumb is to let the soil dry out before you water again. For small plants, let the top couple of inches dry out. For larger plants, let the soil deeper down dry out.

In many gardens, these two rules of thumb translate very loosely into a rough summer watering schedule. It might mean that you will water established plants once or twice per month and young plants every week or two. Successful gardeners fine-tune these very rough schedules based on the plants, on the garden's site, and on the weather.

In their first summer, seedlings and plants with very small roots may need water more frequently. Plants from creeksides and the fog belt, such as leopard lily (*Lilium pardalinum*) and scarlet monkeyflower (*Mimulus cardinalis*), may thrive with more frequent water, while plants from the chaparral, such as flannel bush (*Fremontodendron californicum*) or woolly blue curls (*Trichostema lanatum*), may not tolerate quite so much. Plants with broad and supple leaves, such as western spicebush (*Calycanthus occidentalis*), lose more water through evaporation than those with stiff, small, gray, or fuzzy leaves, such as Cleveland sage (*Salvia clevelandii*). Sandy soil on an open, southern slope—or with reflected heat in an urban setting—dries out faster than clay soil in a sheltered swale. Windy weather also decreases the time it takes for the soil to dry out.

Amid all these variables, the key to getting the frequency right is to check the soil from time to time. Check young plants every few days, since they can dry out and die quickly. In plants newly set out from containers, be sure to check the root ball itself, which may be drier than the surrounding soil. Throughout the garden, the soil may form a little

dry crust on top if there is no mulch. Break through the crust to check for moisture and to water. If the soil is still moist below the crust at the level of the roots, then wait longer before watering. If it is dry, it is safe to give most of the garden another deep soak.

COOL MORNINGS The combination of heat and moisture promotes harmful fungal growth, so water on mild days rather than during heat waves. Water ahead of forecasted Santa Anas, instead of waiting until the hot, dry winds blast us. Water in the cool of the morning instead of during the heat of the afternoon. Despite California's generally cool nights, stick to the morning routine, particularly if you use overhead sprinklers or hose off the plants. Water sits longer on the plants at night, giving fungi more time to mount an attack. Some of our most xeric plants suffer most

Streamside plants, such as leopard lily (left), benefit from regular water, while woolly blue curls and sulfur buckwheat (right) do not.
STEPHEN INGRAM

JUNE

127

from night watering because—unlike most plants—they open their pores at night.

DO NOT OVERWATER In most of the state, summer water wreaks havoc with life underground. Not only does overwatering in the warmth of the summer promote the growth of fungal pathogens that lead to root rot and crown rot, it also harms beneficial fungi. Native plants have evolved with soil fungi that link to their roots and enable them to take in nutrients and water efficiently. These links, called mycorrhizal links, enable plants to ward off diseases, help them recover from drought, and improve the structure of the soil. The mycorrhizae exist in mature native gardens, but they take time to develop in transitional gardens. Overwatering (or overfertilizing) disrupts the establishment of these unseen but important underground relationships.

Overwatering also causes other problems. It needlessly encourages weeds and garden pests, such as aphids and gophers. In the parts of the state where irrigation water contains salts, watering during the dry season also causes salt to build up in the soil. While it is tempting to provide extra water for faster growth, hold off for now. Instead, water the soil deeply for survival, and hose off the plants once a month for looks. Irrigate, if you like, to stretch the natural rainy season forward a bit in fall and to push it out a bit in spring, but use restraint in summer.

Check, Repair, and Adjust Irrigation

Watering mechanisms can be as simple as a hose, or they can involve complex piping and carefully engineered rotators. Whatever mechanism you have chosen, it must work. Kinked hoses, clogged emitters, and punctured lines can mean too little water in one location and too much elsewhere. Both cause trouble in summer. Inspect the watering system while it is running to make sure the water is arriving where it is needed. If you have buried hoses or tubes under mulch, lift the mulch to inspect the hoses and the soil. Look for dry patches and look for puddles, large or small. Repair, alter, or replace what is not working.

Even when an irrigation system works as originally planned, it needs adjustment as the garden changes each season. As your plants grow, move hoses, drippers, or sprinklers farther away from them. This will encourage their roots to stretch. If mulch has accumulated in your garden, check to make sure that it is doing its job of keeping the soil moist and not acting as a barrier that keeps water out. If you use an automated watering system, lengthen the interval between waterings as the plants mature. Consider leaving the system on a manual setting so you will be sure to water only when needed.

Clean Up Shrubs, Groundcovers, and Perennials

Several shrubs, groundcovers, and perennials flower in late spring and can be pruned now. For some, pruning now simply means a bit of pinching or deadheading. The beautiful blooms of tree anemone (*Carpenteria californica*) do not age well, so deadhead them to keep them tidy and pinch them to keep them full. Remove the seeds of island snapdragon (*Galvezia speciosa*), if you do not like them, or leave them for the birds. Deadhead coyote mint (*Monardella villosa*), monkeyflower (*Mimulus* spp.), and penstemon (*Penstemon* spp.). Use a light touch on the monkeyflower: it doesn't regenerate well from old wood. Penstemon stalks, on the other hand, can be cut back to the ground. Mow purple needlegrass (*Nassella pulchra*) when it goes dormant. This is also the time to pinch, or even edge, low-growing manzanita (*Arctostaphylos* spp.) if you would like fuller foliage. If fire is a real risk, then it is also time to use a string trimmer on spent annuals.

For many other plants, this month's pruning entails only the removal of deadwood and, occasionally, a few selected branches. Removing deadwood improves the look of most shrubs, it may improve their health, and it decreases the fire load. Take a fresh look at your shrubs when the deadwood is gone. Both redshank (*Adenostoma sparsifolium*) and chamise (*A. fasciculatum*) form broad billowy outlines, but either can be thinned now to a more fountain-like shape, which suits many garden settings. You might even transform a redshank into a multi-trunked tree to enjoy the bark's ruddy ribbons. To renew tall Oregon grape (*Berberis* spp.), remove some of the old branches that have lost their lower leaves. For large, mature manzanita, selective pruning—when done thoughtfully and infrequently—can reveal its beautiful bark and branching structure.

Where summers are intense, make only a few major cuts to old manzanita in any single year. Your restraint will allow the inner branches to gradually adapt to the increase in sunlight.

Take Cuttings

It is not too late to propagate wild mock orange (*Philadelphus lewisii*) and golden currant (*Ribes aureum*) from cuttings if you didn't start them in May. You also can take root crown cuttings from Pacific dogwood (*Cornus nuttallii,* which also can be layered) or stem cuttings from red elderberry (*Sambucus racemosa*), toyon (*Heteromeles arbutifolia*), big-leaf maple (*Acer macrophyllum*), and creek dogwood (*Cornus sericea*). For stem cuttings, use pieces that are about four inches long and strip off the lower leaves before you strike them into the rooting medium. Mild rooting hormone improves their success. Keep the cuttings moist and protected from sun, wind, and animals. (For more tips on growing successful cuttings, see November, pages 35–37.) When the plants show signs of growth on top, the roots have developed and it is time to pot them up. If they grow vigorously in their pots, they will be ready to set out in the garden by mid-fall.

Solarize a Lawn

If you would like to replace all or part of a lawn with natives, you must first kill the lawn. In a sunny area, you can solarize it. That is, you can cover the lawn with clear plastic film for a month or so in summer, and let the heat of the sun kill it. The long days of June heat up inland areas, where solarization works best.

Like a greenhouse, the plastic sheet lets in the sun's rays and traps the heat. The soil heats up best when the plastic lies right against it, so aim for an even ground surface under the plastic. Mow the lawn down close to the ground first, and leave the clippings in place. Some gardeners add an inch or two of organic mulch or compost to smooth over the lawn. Water well, soaking the soil a good foot down; then lay the plastic. If a single sheet is too small, overlap the ends. Bury the outer edges with soil or rocks to keep the plastic firmly in place. A very thin plastic, say one millimeter, works well, though thicker plastic, up to two millimeters, stands up better to wind. Now, simply wait.

In a sunny plot outside of the fog belt, solarized soil temperature will exceed 110° F. and kill most grasses and annual weeds in a month. (For Bermuda grass, which is more difficult to eradicate, some gardeners have had better success with a solid cover of cardboard, overlaid with mulch and left for three months.) Unless you bought UV-rated plastic, it will begin to degrade after about six weeks, so do not leave it on much longer. When you remove the plastic, the soil will be ready for new plantings when you are. In the meantime, sit tight. Turning over the soil or watering it will only allow weeds to take hold. Leave it be (or cover it with mulch) until planting time.

Plant and Sow Where There Is Water

If you plan to water, you can still plant warm-season grasses, such as blue grama (*Bouteloua gracilis*) or purple threeawn (*Aristida purpurea*). Both hail from southern California and are small enough to fit into any garden. Blue grama can be used as a native lawn, though if planted inland it tans up in winter. Purple threeawn provides a nice accent to a border or rock garden. It forms narrow clumps with showy flower spikes. While neither of these grasses needs much water when established, both will need regular water to get started now.

With both water and shade, you can set out redwood or riparian plants, including wild ginger (*Asarum caudatum*) and Pacific bleeding heart (*Dicentra formosa*). As summer's drought takes over, deer venture more into irrigated landscapes to browse. While deer do not bother grasses, they do browse heavily on new leafy growth. Neither wild ginger nor Pacific bleeding heart is a deer favorite. Wild ginger is a lush, almost tropical-looking groundcover. It keeps good company with Pacific bleeding heart, whose pink flowers dangle just above ginger's broad leaves and bleeding heart's own lacy foliage. Whether or not the deer eat your ginger, you should not. Despite its past use and gingery scent, it is now thought to be toxic to humans.

In areas with a bit of high shade, you also can continue to sow some wildflower seeds, such as California bluebells (*Phacelia campanularia*), goldfields (*Lasthenia californica*), and clarkias (*Clarkia* spp.). Like anything planted now, they will need water.

Pacific bleeding heart and other plants that rely on (and get) summer water can be planted now. DEE WONG

WHAT'S IN BLOOM?

The long days of June invite us all outside. Children on summer break, graduates, barbeque companions, and even wedding guests enjoy the garden now, and our native plants adorn it with flowers in every color.

Some of the most alluring blooms are white. Western azalea (*Rhododendron occidentale*) brightens shady glens with familiar fragrant white nosegays. At our feet, fairy lantern (*Calochortus albus*) nods demurely. Ninebark (*Physocarpus capitatus*) proffers dense clusters of white blooms to hold in our hands. Papery-white citrus-scented flowers cover the wild mock orange (*Philadelphus lewisii*). From the backs of beds, stems of ocean spray (*Holodiscus discolor*) arch down, heavy with tiny pink balls that open in a cascade of aromatic white blooms. The flowers of clematis (*Clematis* spp.) dance along fences and arbors. Jumbo fried egg–like flowers blaze raucously from Matilija poppy (*Romneya coulteri*). The creamy white blooms of the blue elderberry (*Sambucus mexicana*) sit up high in flat-topped clusters, presaging the blue berries to come.

For now, the blue hues—along with lavenders—come from sun-loving flowers. Soft blue spires of flowers cover Cleveland sage (*Salvia clevelandii*) for several weeks. Woolly blue curls (*Trichostema lanatum*) bloom vividly all summer, and the warm sun brings out the aroma of their foliage. The daisy-like flowers of Pacific aster (*Aster chilensis*) fill in as groundcover, sporting blue and lavender blooms until fall. California bluebell (*Phacelia campanularia*) is an intensely blue annual, while the flowers of tansy-leaf phacelia (*P. tanacetifolia*) and California phacelia (*P. californica*) are lavender hued.

A few striking June flowers combine hot colors in cool shade. The bright red petals and spurs of western columbine (*Aquilegia formosa*) surround protruding yellow stamens that seem to have been dipped in paint. The orange blooms of our two most recognizable native lilies, Humboldt lily and leopard lily (*Lilium humboldtii* and *L. pardalinum*), are splashed with spots of deep red. Their large, bold blooms hang down from tall stalks.

Reds and pinks come from late-blooming annuals, such as farewell to spring (*Clarkia amoena*) and punch-bowl godetia (*C. bottae*). They come from shrubs such as spicebush (*Calycanthus occidentalis*), which

California bluebells, annuals, bloom with a bush monkeyflower. SAXON HOLT

Red-flowered buckwheat and saffron buckwheat thrive and flower abundantly in rocky soils. SAXON HOLT

offers the whiff of a wine barrel in each burgundy flower. They come from perennials, notably red-flowered buckwheat (*Eriogonum grande* var. *rubescens*), which will bloom through September and carry its decorative seed heads into late fall.

More warm colors come from California poppy (*Eschscholzia californica*) and bush monkeyflower (*Mimulus* spp.). Usually orange, both come in other colors as well, both rebloom when cut back, and both are said to be deer resistant. Yellows come from sulfur buckwheat (*Eriogonum umbellatum*), the continued blooms of island bush poppy (*Dendromecon harfordii*), and tarweed (*Madia elegans*). Sulfur buckwheat is perhaps the most intense yellow, while island bush poppy's yellow is buttery. The cheery yellow tarweed is a reliable summer-blooming annual. Its brightness is made more vivid by its height—it can reach five feet or more. It blooms through morning fog like a smiling face, providing an antidote to the "June gloom" that sometimes shrouds the coast.

Mist and Tinder

July

Cool morning fog rests on the northwest corner of the state. Its gray mist nurses violets (*Viola* spp.), ferns, huckleberries (*Vaccinium ovatum*), and redwoods (*Sequoia sempervirens*). Inland, the sun saturates the day. Most of California is bone dry—tinder for stray sparklers on the Fourth of July. This month, road signs tell campers that the fire danger is high. In dry years, some chaparral plants in the wild lose their leaves now and enter into an early summer dormancy.

Outside the fog belt, relentless dry days remind us that a little water goes a long way in the garden. Some gardeners judiciously water to protect against fire, to keep young plants alive, to forestall summer dormancy, or to perpetuate a private springtime. Many others do not water at all once their gardens become established. Some face water rationing; others do not have the time or inclination to fuss

❮ Succulents, such as this dudleya, are some of the last plants to catch fire. JUDY KRAMER

Garden for fire safety

Wilderness areas carry the threat of wildfire. If you garden near the wilderness, clean up excess "fuel" and maintain an area around your home that includes healthy fire-resistant plants. Include a sizable area with only low-growing plants; this provides a fire break and space for firefighters to do their job.

Pinch and prune

Deadhead perennials and pinch back flowering shrubs. Many evergreen shrubs and trees are susceptible to disease if pruned during the rainy season, so prune them now if they need it.

Plant and sow

Mid-summer is not the traditional time to plant in California, but we can still sow seeds and set out riparian plants and warm-season grasses. We can also sow perennial seeds in containers and they'll be ready to plant out in the fall.

Take cuttings

Gardeners have consistent success with July cuttings of wild mock orange (*Philadelphus lewisii*), salal (*Gaultheria shallon*), and pink-flowering currant (*Ribes sanguineum*). This is also a good time to take cuttings of California hazelnut (*Corylus cornuta* var. *californica*), Dutchman's pipe (*Aristolochia californica*), and monkeyflower (*Mimulus* spp.).

Weed and mulch

Keep after Bermuda grass (*Cynodon dactylon*) and other warm-season weeds. Top off mulch to keep weeds down and to retain moisture (but keep it away from the trunks of trees and shrubs).

Water where it is needed

Water seedlings, newly set out plants, and riparian and redwood understory plants. Water perennials, such as sage (*Salvia* spp.) and buckwheat, on a cool morning to perk them up if needed. If you live in a fire-prone location, water enough to green up the plants closest to your home. If you use an irrigation system, inspect it and repair what is broken.

Do not water where it is not needed

Not all plants need summer water, and some fare poorly when it is given.

with hand-watering or irrigation. Still others eschew watering for aesthetic reasons. Their gardens are designed to embrace the tempo of the seasons, a sense of place, and a particular ideal of beauty. In such gardens, we savor the spare and rugged drama of a dry California summer.

NATIVE GARDENING IN JULY
Garden for Fire Safety

The California wilderness is vast and beautiful. Nearby gardens borrow from its splendor. They share its vistas, its volunteer seedlings, and its wildlife. They also share its threat of wildfire. Gardening near wilderness means gardening with fire in mind.

While the state's most devastating fires often occur in fall, the fire season officially begins each spring, and by now most wilderness areas display the gray-green and gold mosaic of summer. Close to home, the summer-dry mosaic must be managed for safety in a wildfire. Garden landscapes must slow the feeding of a fire as it nears and starve it when it gets really close. A managed garden will not stop a fire, but it will check its pace and give firefighters the time and space they need to do their work.

REDUCE "FUEL" Fire safety starts with ordinary garden cleanup to reduce fuel. Remove accumulated leaves and needles from the roof and gutters, and from where they have eddied up in courtyard corners. If you haven't already done so, string trim or mow spent annuals and dry grasses to four inches (but not to bare ground, which is susceptible to erosion). Take away fallen twigs and built-up leaf litter and pine needles, leaving just the bottom few inches of duff. Now is a good time to prune scrub and chaparral plants. Remove dead limbs and reduce the volume that would feed a fire. Clear away dead plants, but leave their roots intact to keep the soil stable. Keep the living plants near your home green and healthy. Even many drought-tolerant plants need a little water to stay green enough to resist burning.

You also may need to remove some living plants. Pepper tree (*Schinus* spp.), acacia (*Acacia* spp.), and upright rosemary (*Rosmarinus officinalis*) are nonnatives with flammable oils or fine, dry branches and leaves that ignite easily. Some native plants, including chamise (*Adenostoma fasciculatum,* known tellingly as greasewood in some areas) and California sagebrush (*Artemisia californica*), also are flammable. None of these belongs alongside your home. A few nonnative invasive plants, such as pampas and jubata grass (*Cortaderia selloana* and *C. jubata*), many types of eucalyptus (*Eucalyptus* spp.), and Scotch broom (*Cytisus scoparius*), pose a special problem. Their uninterrupted spread and heavy buildup of litter feed intense, dangerous fires.

TRIM TREES Fire climbs through trees to buildings and to the roof. Keep tree branches from touching buildings and decks. If large trees are near the house, consider removing limbs that may be below the level of the roof, particularly if they are under eaves. The low limbs carry fire

Limbed-up oaks and a well-groomed garden reduce the risk of fire. SAXON HOLT

from the ground to their canopies and to the roof (which should be made of fire-resistant material). Farther from the house, consider removing limbs below six feet. With its reliably dry weather, July is an ideal month to prune the low limbs of many evergreen oaks, such as coast, interior, and canyon live oak (*Quercus agrifolia, Q. wislizenii,* and *Q. chrysolepsis*), as well as black oak (*Q. kelloggii*). These trees are all slow to ignite and slow to burn. They are even more resilient when they are limbed up.

PROVIDE SPACE The next step is to judiciously remove some shrubs and trees to create or preserve open spaces between plants, between planting areas, and between plants and buildings. A fire will slow its pace or even exhaust itself if it has to jump a wide stretch before reaching more fuel. Vertical distance also matters. Empty space between the tops of shrubs and the lower limbs of trees will slow or prevent a ground fire's climb. One rule of thumb is to provide horizontal open spaces of ten to twenty feet (more on a slope) and vertical distances equal to about three times the height of the shrubs. These gaps will break a fire's pace.

When you do remove plants, look for nesting birds and other wildlife. They may help you choose which plants to keep and which to clear. Where you do clear, consider adding an inch or two of mulch—perhaps the chippings of the removed shrubs—or replanting with low-growing, fire-resistant natives. Mulch and plants both help keep flammable weeds at bay and the soil structure stable.

Suitable natives for planting in the gaps include succulents, such as stonecrop (*Sedum spathulifolium*) and dudleya (*Dudleya* spp.), and other low-growers that accumulate little litter, such as yerba buena (*Satureja douglasii*), blue-eyed grass (*Sisyrinchium bellum*), iris (*Iris* spp. flowers are usually purple, but *I. douglasiana* 'Canyon Snow' has white flowers), strawberry (*Fragaria* spp.), and the low forms of kinnikinnick (*Arctostaphylos uva-ursi*). Plants can be added in the fall, or earlier if water is available. Avoid the most invasive of the nonnative groundcovers. English ivy (*Hedera helix*) and ice plant (*Carpobrotus edulis*) are particularly troublesome. In addition to crowding out native plants, ivy's green cover often masks a thick buildup of dead fuel below, and the shallow roots and heavy weight of ice plant contribute to erosion. Many chapters of the California Native

Low and filled with moisture, stonecrop—like other succulents—resists fire. HELEN POPPER

Plant Society provide lists of fire-resistant natives that are appropriate in gardens close to local wilderness areas.

Pinch and Prune

With or without the threat of fire, most gardens benefit from at least some deadheading, pinching, and pruning this month. We may deadhead for repeat blooms or pinch for shape, snipping ends of shrubs to replicate a deer's browsing, or we may thin shrubs. After a time, some large shrubs can become surprisingly dark and impenetrable. In addition to reducing the fuel load, thinning them a bit lets us enjoy their structure and the play of light they can bring to the garden. It also lets understory plants find enough light to grow.

DEADHEAD PERENNIALS While you may decide to let some perennials go to seed, either for seed collection or for wildlife value, you may want to deadhead others. If so, cut their stems back to the set of leaves just below the spent blooms. Freely deadhead coyote mint (*Monardella villosa*), lilac verbena (*Verbena lilacina*), monkeyflowers (*Mimulus* spp.), penstemons (*Penstemon* spp.), poppies (*Eschscholzia californica*), and sages (*Salvia* spp.). All respond well, either with renewed blooms or with more shapely forms. You might even lightly shear coyote mint and sage (without cutting into old wood) to keep them full.

TIP PINCH SHRUBS Some shrubs send out new growth beyond their flowers and will fill out more if they are pinched back after flowering. Simply use your fingers to pinch off the tips of stems. Once the terminal buds are removed, the plant will redirect growth to the remaining side buds. Pinch back ceanothus (*Ceanothus* spp.) occasionally as you walk through your garden if you would like to encourage dense growth. Now through September is the best time to shape them more, if that is needed. Wild mock oranges (*Philadelphus lewisii*) also respond well to tip pinching, and mature plants can handle extensive thinning or even coppicing. Since they bloom on the recent year's growth, prune them now, after their recent flowering, so you can enjoy fresh blooms next year. Young flannel bushes (*Fremontodendron* spp.) can be tip pinched now, but older ones should be left alone if possible.

PRUNE SHRUBS AND TREES Many versatile native shrubs can be pruned now to take a variety of forms. Wax myrtle (*Myrica californica*), holly-leaf cherry (*Prunus ilicifolia*), Nevin's barberry (*Berberis nevinii*), sugar bush (*Rhus ovata*), and lemonade berry (*R. integrifolia*) can be thinned, shaped into small trees, or clipped into hedges. (Wax myrtle and holly-leaf cherry can even be sheared as topiary.) For healthy hedges, keep the top narrower than the bottom. Tapering them will let light reach the wider bottom branches.

Shaping shrubs into trees calls for the reverse: let the upper branches widen, and remove the lower stems as they become shaded. While lower stems are still small and receiving light, leave them in place to help the plant grow. Remove them gradually, but do so before they become substantial in size and heavily shaded.

Other shrubs that can be pruned now include toyon (*Heteromeles arbutifolia*), coffeeberry (*Rhamnus californica*), Oregon grape (*Berberis* spp.), and manzanita (*Arctostaphylos* spp.). Toyon and coffeeberry can be pruned to encourage a particular shape, to let in more light, or to limit their size. Oregon grape benefits from having old canes removed. Many large manzanitas are best left untouched for years at a stretch, and branches that are trimmed back beyond healthy growth will not recover. Nevertheless, with restraint they can be pruned now to remove deadwood or reveal their bark and structure.

Many native evergreen trees are particularly susceptible to disease if cuts are made during wet weather, so now is a good time to prune them if they need it. Evergreen oaks (*Quercus* spp.), junipers (*Juniperus* spp.), and cypresses (*Cupressus* spp.) can all be pruned now.

Experienced gardeners remove dead, damaged, and diseased limbs before making any cuts for aesthetics, and they do not top trees or leave

Bigberry manzanita (*Arctostaphylos glauca*) and other chaparral plants can be pruned now. STEPHEN INGRAM

other stubs. When large trees (especially oaks) need trimming, most experienced gardeners also know to hire well-recommended certified arborists to do the job safely and leave them with healthy trees.

Plant and Sow

While summer is not California's traditional planting season, you still can sow and plant anything that tolerates and will receive summer water. Riparian and redwood understory plants, as well as many grasses, can be sown or planted now. Some professional landscapers who use carefully designed irrigation consider summer to be a good time to establish a native lawn. There is ample daylight for germination, and with water a lawn can come in quickly from seed. Now is also a good time to sow perennial seeds in containers for fall planting.

Take Cuttings

Gardeners have had consistent success with mid-summer tip cuttings of wild mock orange (*Philadelphus lewisii*), monkeyflower (*Mimulus* spp.), and salal (*Gaultheria shallon*), and some success with cuttings of Dutchman's pipe (*Aristolochia californica*) taken farther back on the stem. Use cuttings from new, non-flowering growth that has firmed up. Letting the new growth firm up a bit first may make the cuttings slower to root, but it also makes them less likely to rot. While it is important to keep the cuttings moist and cool, it is also important not to go overboard misting them,

The author uses cuttings to get more of an unusually colored monkeyflower.
HELEN POPPER

especially the mock orange, which rots easily. (For more on stem cuttings, see the discussion in November, pages 35–37.)

From mid-July until mid-August, semi-hardwood cuttings of pink-flowering currant (*Ribes sanguineum*) root reliably; they can then be potted up in fall. Cuttings of California hazelnut (*Corylus cornuta* var. *californica*) are a bit more difficult. Perhaps only half of them will take, but now through early fall is the best time to try semi-hardwood cuttings. If successful, they will be ready to put into containers in September. Rooting hormone improves the odds for alder (*Alnus* spp.) as well as for other July cuttings.

Weed and Mulch

Where gardens receive little water, gardeners can slacken their pace of weeding this month. Bermuda grass (*Cynodon dactylon*) and a few other warm-season weeds are problems, but without water most weeds slow down, and we can follow suit. Where water is abundant, weeds will continue to germinate and grow, so the job continues.

Lighten your weeding chores by using liberal amounts of mulch. In woodland gardens, leaf litter and bark work well. In chaparral and scrub, gravel or decomposed granite works better. Move mulch away from the base of plants if it has piled up there, and top off bare spots elsewhere. Mulch will also help retain moisture, making watering less of a chore too.

Water Where It Is Needed

Despite having evolved in a Mediterranean climate, many California natives need water in the summer. Riparian plants, and even valley and desert plants—ones that are used to heat, but not complete summer drought—expect some water. Keep in mind there is a difference between heat tolerance and drought tolerance. In addition, seedlings and new plants need it even if they will be drought tolerant once established, so water new plantings this month. Water them slowly, and let the water soak in enough to go beyond the reach of their roots. Then, unless they hail from wet areas, let them dry out before you water them again.

Even some established drought-tolerant native plants look more garden worthy if they are watered once a month. Established sages (*Salvia* spp.) and most buckwheats (*Eriogonum* spp.), for example, can survive without summer water, but they are prettier with a few waterings each summer. If you can spare the time and water, go ahead and give them a deep, slow soak this month. To minimize the chance of losses to fungal disease, water in the morning, on a relatively cool day.

If you rely on an irrigation system, look for tiny pools of water, dry patches, and soggy soil. One month, emitters pop off. Another month, dirt clogs them. The next month, rodents chew through plastic pipes. Repair what is broken, or turn it off and water with a garden hose. Systems require inspection and maintenance.

Finally, near wilderness areas, fire safety requires that plants close to your home stay green enough to slow a fire. For many drought-tolerant species, such as dudleya and iris under the shade of oaks, that may mean only once a month. However, other species require more frequent irrigation to keep from drying out. Fire safely requires judicious use of water.

Do Not Water Where It Is Not Needed

Summer water promotes weeds, deer browsing, and fungal pathogens. Established evergreen oaks (*Quercus* spp.), flannel bushes (*Fremontodendron californicum*), woolly blue curls (*Trichostema lanatum*), and many types of manzanitas (*Arctostaphylos* spp.) are especially vulnerable to fungal disease. The soil around them should not be allowed to stay moist in summer. Likewise, do not water where dormant bulbs of mariposa lilies and fairy lanterns (*Calochortus* spp.) lie. Dry summer is their time for rest.

WHAT'S IN BLOOM?

The entrance to a dry garden in the San Gabriel Mountains grabs our attention with a large, showy flannel bush (*Fremontodendron californicum*). It brims high and wide with blazing yellow blooms. More yellow beckons us farther into the garden, where we meet the intense flowers of sulfur buckwheat (*Eriogonum umbellatum*). The blue-purple blooms of coyote mint (*Monardella villosa*) provide a cheerful complement, and local pink mariposa lilies (*Calochortus palmeri*) pop up to surprise us. Their unusual color is subtly echoed in the blush of California's native perennial morning glory (*Calystegia macrostegia*), which twines in the background.

In a coastal garden, undulating rows of sea pinks (*Armeria maritima*) embrace a breakfast patio. Their flowers stand like pink lollipops on tidy green mounds. Nearby masses of lilac-blue Pacific asters (*Aster chilensis*) invite endless games of "he loves me, he loves me not." Behind them, late-sown tidy-tips (*Layia platyglossa*), bird's-eye gilias and globe gilias (*Gilia tricolor* and *G. capitata*), and Pismo clarkias (*Clarkia speciosa* ssp. *immaculata*) fill the scene with waves of yellow, blue, and pink.

Summer is still new to portions of the state's upper reaches, and the flower displays there evince its later arrival. In a cool northern glade, the delicate white blooms of California lady's slippers (*Cypripedium californicum*) entice us with their fragrance. Leopard lilies (*Lilium pardalinum*) tower

Monkeyflower and coyote mint bloom together in the Santa Cruz Mountains.

dramatically behind them; their orange and yellow flowers hang like pendants from six-foot stalks. Along the garden's path, the tiny, bright flowers of yellow-eyed grass (*Sisyrinchium californicum*) seem to wink at us, and Pacific bleeding hearts (*Dicentra formosa*) still dangle. Beyond them, elegant brodiaeas (*Brodiaea elegans*) decorate a postage-stamp meadow of diminutive perennial bunchgrasses. The path ends at a small pond. On one side, stream orchids (*Epipactis gigantea*) bloom amidst cobra lilies (*Darlingtonia californica*), our state's strange carnivores. On the other side, a swath of scarlet monkeyflowers (*Mimulus cardinalis*) follows the pond's curve. A western azalea (*Rhododendron occidentale*) rises up behind it, and a few luminous white blooms still reflect in the water below.

Western azalea's beautiful blooms are also scented.

RENATE KEMPF

Siesta Time

August

Rest in the shade of an oak, a redwood, or a bay. With eyelids resting too, enjoy the unseen pleasures of a summer's day. Inhale the thick scent of pitcher sage (*Lepechinia fragrans*) or the piquancy of yerba buena (*Satureja douglasii*). Let the breeze borrow the fragrance and gently set it down again. Hear a calling quail, and another, the rustle of a darting lizard, and the sudden quiet that follows.

Later, open your eyes to see pieces of cerulean sky framed by branches. Lower your gaze. Perhaps ripe blackberries, thimbleberries, or huckleberries (*Rubus ursinus, R. parviflorus,* or *Vaccinium ovatum*) will awaken your appetite. Yield to what you see. Taste a berry, crush a leaf, pick a flower. You'll see an occasional weed too, or a monkeyflower that would look prettier trimmed back. You might decide to prune some tangled branches from a small tree, or even—

❮ Sunflowers bloom all summer. JUDY KRAMER

Water

Containers, seedlings, and young plants all dry out quickly, so check them regularly to see if they need water. If riparian and other moisture-loving plants don't get water from fog, streams, or seeps, give them a drink. For other plants, let the soil dry out completely between waterings.

Plant and propagate, a little

With adequate water, moisture-loving plants can be divided and put in the ground almost any time, including now.

Prune

This is the season in which many evergreen plants slow their growth or go dormant. It is a good time to cut back and clean up many perennials and cool-season grasses, and it is also an appropriate time to prune evergreen shrubs and trees.

Harvest fresh berries

Huckleberries, thimbleberries, and California blackberries (*Vaccinium ovatum, Rubus parviflorus,* and *R. ursinus*) are ready to eat. Blue elderberries (*Sambucus mexicana*) are ready to use in preserves.

Weed

Most weeds have slowed their pace, especially in dry gardens. However, in northern and central California, Himalayan blackberry remains a problem. If you plan to use herbicide to help eradicate it, now is a good time to do it.

Embrace the "fifth season"

Enjoy the garden's summer textures, sounds, and smells. In most of California, this is the garden's slow season. Relish it.

with sufficient moisture—divide some sedges. There are still a few chores to pry a gardener, when ready, away from a summer siesta.

NATIVE GARDENING IN AUGUST
Water

If you are nursing along container plants, perhaps for fall planting, be sure to water them attentively and provide some shade as well. Containers— especially black nursery pots— heat up and dry out quickly. Plants in the ground also benefit from having cool roots. Rocks or other mulch can help keep their water demands low. Water seedlings, new plantings, and moisture-loving plants. Let the water flow slowly, so it will reach deep into the soil without running off. Unless your garden includes plants that need constant moisture, let the soil dry out between waterings.

Cool mornings are the best time to water. There is less evaporation when it is cool, and for plants that are susceptible to fungal attack, the risk of that is lower in the morning. During hot spells, be careful not to leave wet soil under established summer-dry plants, especially such favorites as flannel bushes (*Fremontodendron californicum*), woolly blue curls (*Trichostema lanatum*), and evergreen oaks (*Quercus* spp.). For these, you might skip watering altogether. If you do water them, water out at the drip line, where rain might naturally fall—well away from the base of the plant. Do not water summer-dry bulbs, such as goldenstars (*Bloomeria crocea*) and most brodiaeas (*Brodiaea* spp.) and wild onions (*Allium* spp.). In addition to keeping these plants healthy, withholding water where it isn't needed also helps shrink weeding chores.

Plant and Propagate, a Little

While this is not the traditional planting time, any plants that rely on summer water can still be planted now. You also can divide riparian plants, such as sedges, as long as you keep them moist. Division exposes the roots even more than planting from a container, so watering them well, both before and after division, is important.

Prune

Pruning needs have a way of accumulating. By late summer, trees and shrubs may be cluttered with tangled interior wood or dead limbs. Perennials may look haggard. Cool-season grasses may have built up a bit too much thatch. The near dormancy of many plants and the completion of so many birds' nesting cycles nudge us now toward the loppers and secateurs. Garden pruning replaces with a tame hand the work of herbivores in the wild and of fire in the past. (Both Native Americans and early ranchers historically used fire to improve their yields.) Consider pruning some of your own natives now, the ones near dormancy. You also may want to prune your nonnative plants, to keep them in balance with the rest of your garden.

TREES AND SHRUBS Cleaning up trees and large shrubs is important in the south, where the Santa Ana winds will pick up as early as September. Up north, it will be important soon after, when heavy storms arrive. Pruning now will give wounds time to heal before the rainy season begins.

With an eye out for nesting birds in every cranny, clear debris and dead branches from oaks, such as Engelmann's oak, coast live oak, scrub oak, and leather oak (*Quercus engelmannii, Q. agrifolia, Q. berberidifolia,* and *Q. durata*). The small scrub and leather oaks can be opened up a bit to reveal their captivating branching structure. It is also a good time to prune Catalina ironwood (*Lyonothamnus floribundus*) and bay (*Umbellularia californica*). Remove the suckers from ironwood if you would like to keep it as a single-trunked tree. Pinch back the tips of the bay if you would like to keep it bushy or small. (If you use the clipped leaves for cooking, use less than you would of traditional bay, *Laurus nobilis.*) Or thin a few of the young lower branches of the bay to give it an open form. For large trees, use a certified arborist. Good arborists know what's best for the tree itself and for what it provides to the habitat of the garden.

Many chaparral shrubs are best pruned now. The dry days of August found in most of the state provide the best insurance against dieback, which is spread by fungus. It is particularly troublesome for ceanothus (*Ceanothus* spp.), which suffers from it when branches more than an inch thick are cut and suffers even more when the weather is wet. Other shrubs

Typically, three cuts are used to prune branches thicker than one and a half inches. First, a partial cut is made on the underside of the branch to stop any possible ripping that might occur as the limb detaches when the full cut is made. Second, shown at left, a complete cut is made farther out from the undercut. Finally, shown at right, the remaining stub is cut back to just outside of the branch collar. HELEN POPPER

are more robust to pruning. For mallow (*Lavatera* spp.), reach into the center to remove unwanted stems down low, near the base. Leave in place the major trunks or the well-placed stems that are to become trunks. Chamise (*Adenostoma fasciculatum*) can be used as topiary, or opened up by removing dead or crisscrossing inner branches.

PERENNIALS Most perennials need some attention from time to time to look their best. Deadhead California aster (*Lessingia filaginifolia*) for continued bloom, or prune it back hard if it is getting leggy. If it has died off at the center, coppicing may revive it. Bush monkeyflower (*Mimulus* spp.) benefits from more modest pruning. Cut it only as far back as there are signs of fresh growth. Cut coyote mint (*Monardella villosa*) back by half or two-thirds every year or two. (If it breaks your heart to cut it back hard, then cut back every other plant.) Lilac verbena (*Verbena lilacina*) is amenable to shears. Cut it back to a dense mound or thin it to a billowy fountain.

Clean up the dead material from other perennials all around the garden unless it is providing needed shade. If it's not too hot and you like a very tidy garden, take out your shears and cut the brown stems and leaves from

Late summer is the time to renew cool-season grasses. A blue fescue (a nonnative mistakenly planted in a native garden) is pictured here in spring with native checkerbloom and iris.

SAXON HOLT

the Douglas iris (*Iris douglasiana*). Resist the temptation to simply pull the leaves from the base; they do not detach readily.

To renew cool-season grasses for the coming season, cut them back, mow them, or rake them out. Red fescue (*Festuca rubra*), Torrey's melic (*Melica torreyana*), needlegrass (*Nassella* spp.), and California bottlebrush grass (*Elymus californicus*) can all be mown or cut with a string trimmer. If you are using a typical lawn mower, put it on the tallest setting. (Some gardeners swap out their mowers' wheels for extra large ones to get sufficient height.) Brown sedge (*Carex subfusca*) can also be cut back now.

WAIT FOR WINTER Dormancy generally is a good guide to the timing of pruning. Do not be tempted to prune most winter deciduous plants now (unless you want to tame their overall growth). Not only is winter a more appropriate time in terms of the plant's health, the lack of leaves allows the plant's structure to guide your pruning.

CLEAN YOUR TOOLS Keep your pruning tools clean and sharp. Well-maintained tools will make your gardening chores easier and safer, and they will keep your plants healthier. Most importantly, wash off the physical remnants of sick plants. If it is necessary to sanitize your tools, use alcohol or mild household cleaners, not bleach, which pits metal. The pits provide tiny protected homes to the very pathogens we try to clean away. Finally, dry your tools before you store them.

Harvest Fresh Berries

Early this month, gardeners and hikers alike enjoy ripe huckleberries (*Vaccinium ovatum*), thimbleberries (*Rubus parviflorus*), and California blackberries (*R. ursinus*). Blue elderberries (*Sambucus mexicana*) are made into wine, and all are preserved in jams and jellies.

Huckleberries and thimbleberries are lovely garden shrubs. Plump, dark blue, and round, huckleberry fruits are similar to blueberries, their traditional cousins. The shrubs are well behaved and evergreen, with small leaves that emerge bronze and mature to a glossy green. The plants are most at home on the North and Central Coast, but they also pop up in the higher elevations inland and in southern California. On the North Coast, they are so common that you can find huckleberry preserves in local shops. In your own garden, you can enjoy the berries immediately as you pick them at the bush, or you can carry them inside to share in a fruit salad or jam.

Thimbleberries are like flat, tart raspberries. The berry season overlaps with the pretty rose-like flowers. Individual berries go from firm to ripe quickly, sometimes in just an afternoon. The plants come from moist areas: woodlands, stream banks, meadows, and even (pioneer plants that they are) roadside gullies. Because they rely on water all summer, they can still be put into the ground now. While they can grow rampantly, they grow easily to a modest size, and they have no thorns. Their lovely felted young leaves mature to a smooth soft green, then change to gold before they drop in fall.

Native blackberry and elderberry both require a bit more room but can get by with much less moisture. Both have been ripening since midsummer, and they still abound. The native blackberry grows in many habitats, as does the aggressive nonnative Himalayan blackberry (*Rubus discolor*). The troublesome nonnative has stiff, angular canes, with stout and often hooked thorns. It is disruptive in the wild and in the garden, and it is hard to get rid of. Our tamer native, with suppler canes and softer spines, makes a more manageable garden plant and provides useful habitat. Its berries are smaller but delicious fresh and in cobblers and pies.

Blue elderberries are large shrubs that sometimes grow as multi-trunked trees. They are often found near blackberries in the wild, and the two make good garden companions where there is room for both. Elderberries sprawl a bit, with many woody stems. They are especially nice on the low end of a slope, where their masses of flowers and berries—and the wildlife they draw—can be viewed from above. Cook their berries, then use them to make pies or jellies or wine.

Weed

Most weeding jobs slow down this month. The key exception in northern and central California is the Himalayan blackberry (*Rubus discolor*), which invades both gardens and wilderness. If left unchecked it can easily overrun even the largest gardens, and it is hard to get rid of. Besides having tough thorns, the canes regrow vigorously from the root crown after being cut back. Cutting must be continually repeated or combined with removal of the root crown or use of an herbicide (such as glyphosate).

Once the berries have been produced, the plant sends energy to its roots. This means that the roots will take up whatever herbicide you apply now through early fall. (If you apply it too early, it will kill the foliage but not the root.) Wet the foliage well with a heavy concentrate of herbicide and expect a few weeks to pass before you can see it doing its job. After a month or two, cut back whatever canes do grow back. If it is a particularly dry year, less herbicide will make it to the roots, so you will have to rely more on manual work. If you already cut the brambles back hard earlier in the year, then don't wait for the berries before applying the herbicide. New canes don't produce berries, and the plant begins earlier to send energy back to the roots.

Once you have diminished the bramble, you can further subdue it by using other plants to shade it out. If the bramble is too large to tackle in one season, begin at the outer edges, where its hold is weakest. You can push it back there to establish and protect your garden.

Embrace the "Fifth Season"

"The dry season is California's winter," wrote David Rains Wallace in his 1987 essay "The Fifth Season." He called on Californians to embrace this fragile time of year. Decades later, Judith Larner Lowry helped many California gardeners to do just that. In her sensitive book *The Landscaping Ideas of Jays*, she writes of the tranquil beauty of Wallace's "fifth season." She reminds us that in a native garden, the warm days that blend late summer and early fall comprise a time apart—a slow time. In the garden, it is a season of quiet, of scent, of sun-ripened berries, of small tasks, and of rest. It is a season to enjoy.

WHAT'S IN BLOOM?

While August is the slow, retiring season for many of California's native plants, we can still find flowers for the garden. Some species husband what scant water they find and use it to bloom profusely. Others succeed by growing near water, and they demand it in the garden. With only a small share of native plants flowering in the wild this month, butterflies, birds, bees, and moths all find their way to what blooms in our gardens.

Butterflies rely heavily on natives in the sunflower family, including sunflowers (*Helianthus annuus*) themselves, goldenrods (*Solidago californica*), gumplants (*Grindelia stricta*), and asters (*Lessingia filaginifolia* and *Aster chilensis*). Our classic yellow annual sunflower feeds them straight through fall, and its tall stalks make great cut flowers. Goldenrods, true to their name, attract butterflies with long plumes of gold, and gumplants provide a bright yellow mat. California asters (*Lessingia filaginifolia*) and Pacific asters (*Aster chilensis*) give up their nectar in heaps of pink to lavender-blue ray flowers.

Hummingbirds dart among the fiery trumpets of California fuchsias (*Epilobium* spp.). In the hottest gardens, desert willow trees (*Chilopsis linearis*) provide clouds of tubular blooms for them, while showy four-o'clocks (*Mirabilis multiflora*) lure hawk moths with a musky evening fragrance. Spires of woolly blue curls (*Trichostema lanatum*) draw both hummingbirds and bumblebees; they sip nectar from the fuzzy, deeply pigmented violet flowers. Amid the hum and buzz, resinous leaves give off the scent of summer vacation.

Bees pollinate seep monkeyflowers (*Mimulus guttatus*) in a moist meadow, and western columbine (*Aquilegia formosa*) hosts bees, birds, and butterflies. Other insects pollinate the arresting blooms of leopard lilies (*Lilium pardalinum*) and stream orchids (*Epipactis gigantea*). In a lush, cool redwood forest, the delicate lilac flowers of redwood sorrel (*Oxalis oregana*) attract bees and butterflies; and redwood violets (*Viola sempervirens*), alumroot (*Heuchera micrantha*), and redwood insideout flowers (*Vancouveria planipetala*) bloom nearby. In the dappled shade of a mixed evergreen forest, butterflies visit the small lavender spires of wood mint (*Stachys bullata*) and the soft pink blooms of wood rose (*Rosa gymnocarpa*). Scarlet hips will soon emerge from the summer's rose.

California fuchsia's long tubular flowers lure hummingbirds in late summer. JUDY KRAMER

In an arid garden, fuchsias spill out around boulders, and showy four-o'clocks rise up behind them. BARNEY BARNETT/WILLARD BAY GARDENS

September

School opens, Labor Day comes and goes, but summer clings to September. In the slowly fading season, some gardeners finish pruning chaparral plants and take cuttings of a few evergreen shrubs along the way. Others trim spent perennials and grasses, leaving the clippings in a low pile for hungry birds. Those with seedlings and young plants nurse them along with the water they need. Still others sit back and do nothing but pass the time in leisure before the busier days ahead.

In the warm, dry days that fill most of California, nature only subtly acknowledges the calendar's fall label. A few early migrating birds forage in our gardens for seed; deer browse heavily where they can; and the afternoon's slanting sun hints that dusk begins to inch into the day.

◀ Coyote bush and a bench invite repose. SAXON HOLT

SEPTEMBER'S JOBS

Weed

Weed seeds lie in wait for the first rains. If you plan to sow or plant natives when the rains come, tackle the weed seeds now. Trick them into germinating early by watering, then hoe them down.

Water

September is a dry month in most of the state, so give water to plants that need it. Young plants, container plants, and streamside plants all need water this month.

Prune

Thin top-heavy limbs that would be a threat in heavy winds. Finish any pruning that is needed by chaparral plants, and clean up bunchgrasses if you like a tidier look.

Propagate

Try taking cuttings of evergreen shrubs, such as ceanothus (*Ceanothus* spp.) and tree anemone (*Carpenteria californica*). You can also take cuttings of currant (*Ribes* spp.) and ocean spray (*Holodiscus discolor*).

Plant bulbs

Some bulbs can be planted now, before the rains. This month, plant mariposa lilies and fairy lanterns (*Calochortus* spp.), fawn lilies (*Erythronium* spp.), and leopard lilies (*Lilium pardalinum*). If you have bulbs in pots, check them for viability and for small bulblets to plant anew.

Look into the future

Enjoy sitting out in your garden and daydreaming a bit. See the garden as it is now, and imagine and plan for the changes to come. Mature groundcovers, shrubs, and trees may eventually supplant a young garden's wildflowers, grasses, and other pioneer plants. In an established garden, a lost tree invites new sun-loving plants to succeed it. The fresh pioneers help curb weeds and erosion until succession repeats itself or takes a new turn. A beautiful garden transforms itself into yet another beautiful garden. Let your daydreams and garden plans make the most of the natural progression.

NATIVE GARDENING IN SEPTEMBER

Weed

As mentioned, the key to success with wildflowers is to tackle weeds before you sow the wildflower seeds. If you plan to sow wildflower seeds in fall, now is the time to suppress the weeds. Steel yourself against the seduction of preemergent herbicides: they are likely to stick around long enough to kill your germinating wildflowers right along with the weeds. Instead, water the site now (or wait for rain) so the weeds will germinate. Then hoe the weeds to cut them off just below the soil surface.

For this task, many gardeners like to use a hula hoe, also called a scuffle, action, stirrup, or swivel hoe. The hula hoe cuts with both the push and the pull strokes. The scuffling often brings up more weeds, especially from seeds that respond to light or cultivation. Repeat the water-germinate-hoe process two or three times to subdue the weedy competition before you sow the seeds you want. In your last pass with the hoe, cultivate as shallowly as possible to avoid stimulating more weeds. Your wildflowers will reward you for your effort.

Water

September is typically dry. Check the soil regularly around seedlings, new plants, and container plants. When the soil feels dry below the surface, provide water. Only plants with established roots manage now without moisture. Give periodic water to redwood understory plants, most of which need fog drip, and to other plants that depend on water all summer even when mature. For other established plants, you can withhold water to let the slow season continue, or you can water when temperatures cool, nudging fall forward by stimulating growth with early "rains." Water slowly, especially at first. Gushing water will run off sun-baked soil. Let the water soak in gradually and deeply.

Prune

Consider thinning trees and shrubs with more foliage than their limbs and roots can support. That way the approaching Santa Anas and northwest storm winds can pass through the thinned plants instead of pulling them

over. Many chaparral shrubs, such as lemonade berry (*Rhus integrifolia*) and Nevin's barberry (*Berberis nevinii*), can be pruned now.

You also might trim, rake, or cut back bunchgrasses, such as California fescue (*Festuca californica*), panicgrass (*Panicum acuminatum*), and deer grass (*Muhlenbergia rigens*). Deer grass is particularly versatile. You can trim it now (and collect the trimmings for basket making); you can enjoy it as it is; or you can cut it back in January, just before its new growth. In the meantime, it will gleam in the lowering fall sun and scatter the light with each breeze.

Propagate

September is a good month to take cuttings of many evergreen shrubs, including tree anemone (*Carpenteria californica*), ceanothus (*Ceanothus* spp.), coyote bush (*Baccharis pilularis*), and mountain mahogany (*Cercocarpus betuloides*). Roots will develop in a month or two. It is also a good time to take cuttings of currant (*Ribes* spp.), before it drop its leaves; of ocean spray (*Holodiscus discolor*); and of Dutchman's pipe (*Aristolochia californica*), which is sometimes hard to find in nurseries. (For more on stem cuttings, see the discussion in November, pages 35–37.)

Several perennials, such as California fuchsias (*Epilobium* spp.), monkeyflowers (*Mimulus* spp.), and sages (*Salvia* spp.), will form roots quickly now, but they can be hard to keep alive through winter. If you are pruning them anyway, try the cuttings now, and if they don't make it, you can take fresh cuttings from the new growth in late winter or early spring. Take the cuttings when it is cool, and keep them protected from wind and sun until you put them in the rooting medium. Ziplock bags work well, and a large paper cup or a small bucket with a wet cloth over it also works.

Plant Bulbs

While most native bulbs are planted later in the fall, this month you can plant mariposa lilies and fairy lanterns (*Calochortus* spp.), fawn lilies (*Erythronium* spp.), and leopard lilies (*Lilium pardalinum*), along with

The bulbs of mariposa lilies can be planted now. DEE WONG

trilliums (*Trillium* spp.). If you have been holding your bulbs in containers over the summer, dump out the dirt at the end of the month and check the bulbs. If they have rotted or shriveled, throw them out (and do not reuse the soil). If the bulbs are doing well, you can repot them in the same soil, or you can refresh the soil, keeping in mind that containers need fertilizer, other amendments, or new soil from time to time. If small new bulbs have formed, remove them. Put the bulblets in their own four-inch pots. They will take a few years to bloom, but removing them gives you new plants and is said to invigorate the parent plant.

Look into the Future

A Minnesotan might browse catalogues inside a cozy home in December, perhaps gazing out a frosted window to study the backbone of the dormant garden. Many of us Californians do our daydreaming now, in September, while so much of the garden is resting. Instead of being inside, we might sip lemonade (or iced yerba buena tea) in a shady spot in the garden

The shade of a maturing garden (shown here in spring) allows irises and ferns to begin to supplant poppies, the sun-loving native garden starters.

HELEN POPPER

itself. If there is no shade, we might plan for some with a tree or an arbor of fast-growing native vines, such as virgin's bower or pipestem clematis (*Clematis ligusticifolia* or *C. lasiantha*), island morning glory (*Calystegia macrostegia*), or grape (*Vitis californica*). Imagining such shade, or flowers, or grasses, or berries, we can pat ourselves on the back for doing a garden chore: planning.

While a few gardeners—those in the cool redwoods or with ample moisture from a stream—can plant anytime, the rest of us prune a bit of spring's exuberance and look at the garden's bones. We see the structure of trees, shrubs, and groundcovers. We think about and plan for the future: how our annuals might give way to maturing shrubs and trees, how a sunny opening might become a shady glen, and how particular plants thrive once trees mature.

We smile on our favorite plants, on their scents, colors, and movement, and on the life they support. We daydream about the favorite we don't have. Some of us pore over plant lists from native nurseries, local parks, botanical gardens and societies, and the California Native Plant Society's local chapters. A few chapters even have their fall sales this month, before the October rush. We find plant after plant that delights us. For each, we ask ourselves. Do we have the room? the right soil? the right slope? the right habitat? When the answer is no, we might impulsively struggle to fit them in, or we might content ourselves with enjoying them elsewhere, in a friend's garden or in the wilderness. When the answer is yes, we happily continue our September planning—our September daydreaming.

> Enjoy your rest
> for the days will come
> when winter rains will beckon
> and you must push forth again.
>
> Linda Yamane, *In Full View*, 1995

WHAT'S IN BLOOM?

In this warm month, summer's blooms parade on. The striking spires of woolly blue curls (*Trichostema lanatum*) ascend from well-drained, sunny

Sunflowers bring late summer cheer. STEPHEN INGRAM

slopes. Poppies (*Eschscholzia californica*) and penstemons (*Penstemon* spp.) renew their blooms after shearing. Nursed along with morning fog, pink clarkias (*Clarkia* spp.) and Pacific asters (*Aster chilensis*) brighten coastal gardens; and Hooker's evening primroses (*Oenothera elata*) send up raucous yellow blooms from the damp soil behind a pond.

Yet summer and fall lean on each other now. In one garden, St. Catherine's lace (*Eriogonum giganteum*) displays a flowering white cloud that resounds of summer. In another, the russet mass of seed heads on its cousin, California buckwheat (*E. fasciculatum*), proclaims fall's approach. The abundant red trumpets of California fuchsia (*Epilobium* spp.) blaze throughout the state, while the red hips of roses grow plump and ready to harvest.

In the lowering light of the afternoon, it is the glint of gold that bridges the seasons. Sunny blooms of lizard tail (*Eriophyllum staechadifolium*), gumplant (*Grindelia stricta*), sunflower (*Helianthus* spp.), goldenaster (*Heterotheca sessiliflora*), tarweed (*Madia elegans*), and goldenrod (*Solidago californica*) all carry the flame of summer. In the same harvest hues, sunlit grasses gently remind us of fall's still surreptitious advance.

SEPTEMBER

171

Native Garden Styles

For most native gardeners, thoughts of style come in cycles. Style first matters during a garden's early stages, when we have our hands full with the initial design or restoration. The role of style then gradually fades for a time. As month follows month and year follows year, we focus instead on the individual plants that require our attention. We lose ourselves in the rhythm of their tending. Only when the plants begin to mature or change does the garden reassert itself as a whole. We see the garden anew, and our thoughts return to style.

We sometimes think of native gardens as informal, even wild. To many of us, that is part of their appeal. Yet natives can fit any style. They can fit into a formal garden, a cottage garden, or a modern one. They work well in rock gardens and herb gardens. They even can be used in the style of a Japanese or Persian garden. This chapter suggests some natives for a few styles. The key to using natives in a particular style is to appreciate what the style represents and recognize what aspects of it you most admire. Then you can use the richness of our native flora as both inspiration and ingredient.

A FORMAL GARDEN

Whether grand or modest, the formal garden at its best provides a sense of order and beauty. A formal garden might be compared to a symphony,

❮ Like Japanese cherry blossoms, redbud's flowers embody spring's transience. STEPHEN INGRAM with clear structure, repetition, and variation on a theme. The garden may be an open-air setting for sculpture. Or it may make up a series of outdoor rooms, with one opening onto another, each having its own clear focal point. This style provides a straightforward way to integrate a house and garden with symmetry, balance, and proportion.

The formal garden is typified by an axial plan with geometric plantings and clearly defined borders. Traditionally, clipped hedges or standards flank a central feature, such as a seat, fountain, sculpture, or even a front door. Because clipped hedges and walls are key features of a formal garden, the style is a good accompaniment for a townhouse or other urban home. Groomed groundcovers delineate boundaries clearly, and the plantings often have an architectural quality. Typical plantings include evergreen hedges, circles or rectangles of lawn, geometric beds of color, and axially placed specimen plants. The formal garden balances natural materials with the order of a geometric or architectural layout. The Egyptians, Greeks, Romans, Moors, Italians, and French all made formal gardens. The key to such a garden is a sense of order and structure.

In a formal garden, you might bring in more natives by flanking a door or gate in part shade with a pair of evergreen shrubs, such as California huckleberry (*Vaccinium ovatum*). Huckleberrry has small, glossy leaves and delicate, pale, urn-shaped flowers followed by edible berries. With afternoon sun, a pair of tree anemones (*Carpenteria californica*) might make a good choice. The tree anemone is notable for its abundance of open, cream flowers with a subtle fragrance. It is a more pedestrian shrub when out of bloom, but it is well shaped, with elongated leaves. Its only drawback is that dead leaves cling to it and must be trimmed off for it to look its best. Both shrubs need some water and reasonable drainage. Huckleberry, a redwood understory plant, can take both more shade and more water than the tree anemone.

In full sun, the choice might be one of the many California coffee-berries (*Rhamnus californica,* for example), ceanothus (*Ceanothus* spp.), or manzanitas (*Arctostaphylos* spp.). Coffeeberries have a rounded, naturally geometric form, and there are several dwarf varieties, so they lend themselves to use as a repeated backbone plant in a formal garden. Ceanothus come in even more forms. A few of them grow well near a lawn as long as there is adequate drainage. Manzanitas grow slowly enough to stay as tidy as a formal garden could require. They are not typically lush plants, but they have an architectural quality, and they feature a striking reddish bark and, in winter and early spring, delicate, urn-shaped blooms. Most grow in well-drained soil, but a few, such as Ione manzanita (*Arctostaphylos myrtifolia*), tolerate heavy clay soil. Any of the manzanitas would reward the close inspection that it might receive from a visitor waiting at the front door.

The clipped evergreen hedges of many formal gardens might be interpreted in California with Howard McMinn manzanita (*Arctostaphylos* 'Howard McMinn') for a low hedge, or with the adaptable Sunset manzanita (*A.* 'Sunset') or wax myrtle (*Myrica californica*) for a taller one. The McNab cypress (*Cupressus macnabiana*), holly-leaf cherry (*Prunus ilicifolia*), and toyon (*Heteromeles arbutifolia*) are other native evergreens that can be trimmed into hedges. For a very large hedge, the Lawson cypress (*Chamaecyparis lawsoniana*), also known as Port Orford cedar, has been used in some English formal gardens. In its native habitat in California's northwest, it reaches well over a hundred feet. In a suburban setting it will need a lot of pruning unless you choose one of the many dwarf forms. Where lots are large, it could be used to line both sides of a drive.

Very large formal gardens might include several Lawson cypresses, or some of California's other regal trees, such as incense-cedars (*Calocedrus decurrens*) or valley oaks (*Quercus lobata*). As a tree, the Lawson is common in manicured English and Dutch parks and can be used the same way in California. The incense-cedar is a naturally symmetric, stately tree. It is fragrant, and, despite being at home in the mountains, it tolerates some heat and drought once established. Valley oaks are deciduous and occur naturally only in California. They are native to California's Great Central Valley and Coast Ranges. A pair of valley oaks framing a view would give the feel of an English estate. They grow quickly and are quite large, typically reaching seventy feet. The big-leaf maple (*Acer macrophyllum*) is a somewhat smaller alternative (reaching thirty to fifty feet) that does well with water.

A formal garden's fountain might be surrounded by a crisp circle of clipped sanddune sedge (*Carex pansa*), planted as a lawn. The formality

A young hedge of holly-leaf cherry fits into a formal garden. HELEN POPPER

might be emphasized with paved or gravel paths leading symmetrically away from the fountain. Adjacent flower beds might include annuals and bulbs, or perennials, such as bleeding hearts (*Dicentra formosa*), coral bells (perhaps *Heuchera* 'Canyon Pink' and *H.* 'Canyon Delight'), or rose rock cress (*Arabis blepharophylla*). These all make good bedding plants for the formal garden as long as they are planted in geometric patterns and cut back after blooming. Seating arrangements might look out over the flower beds, or they might act as sculpture, being focal points themselves. Seats might be surrounded by silk-tassel (*Garrya elliptica*), or they might be enhanced with the scented flowers of wild mock orange (*Philadelphus lewisii*) or snowdrop bush (*Styrax redivivus*). The garden's formality can be structured around the beds or around a central axis with a view at the end, perhaps simply of a strategically placed bench, chair, or birdbath.

When all is said and done, it is the arrangement and maintenance of the plants, rather than the choice of plants, that gives the formal garden its distinctive style. Nevertheless, some plants are better suited than others to the formal garden. When looking for native plants to add to a formal garden, look for ones that can be planted or pruned in abstract shapes or that themselves grow naturally into geometric patterns. Focusing on natives provides a restraint that enhances the sense of formality. Whether with natives or not, in a small garden or large, in California or elsewhere, the idea of all this geometry, symmetry, and proportion is to achieve the balance and harmony that epitomize a classical sense of beauty.

A COTTAGE GARDEN

A cottage garden has a romantic sensibility, not an intellectual one. Abundance is its byword. It is jammed with flowering shrubs, perennials, annuals, and vine-covered fences or arbors. The plants tumble out over walkways and flower profusely. The folk music of garden styles, the cottage garden is full of life—alternately nostalgic, bawdy, touching, and cheerful. It is loaded with color and defiant of formality.

Many of California's annuals are just the thing for a cottage garden. Among the easiest to grow and most prolific (in terms of self-sowing) are poppies (*Eschscholzia californica*) and gilias, including globe gilia and bird's-eye gilia (*Gilia capitata* and *G. tricolor*). Familiar to us all, poppies are coveted by English cottage gardeners for their vibrant golden flowers and their pretty fern-like foliage. They grow well in full sun and require little water. With just the scarcest bit of summer water, they will continue to bloom even into August. They are jauntily complemented by the pale blue of globe gilias. Both gilias flourish in the same conditions as poppies.

Many native perennials have long blooming periods fit for a cottage garden. Two of the easiest to grow are Pacific aster (*Aster chilensis*) and California fuchsia (*Epilobium* spp., still fondly known to many as *Zauschneria*). The Pacific aster takes garden water and has daisy-like flowers that look as if they've been drawn for a storybook. The California fuchsia is yet another hummingbird magnet. It has bright orange-red tubular flowers and silvery-green foliage. It grows in full sun with little to no water and fills in quickly, but unattended it can get scraggly after a few years. Don't be daunted, there's an easy fix: mow it to the ground every year or two once it is established. It will grow back lushly in a few months. Both Pacific aster and California fuchsia flower in late summer and early autumn, when so much else is spent.

Other good choices include monkeyflower, penstemon, and buckwheat. Red bush monkeyflower (*Mimulus puniceus*), like California fuchsia, has bright red tubular flowers that draw hummingbirds. It hails from the south, grows to two to three feet, and flowers from late spring through summer. Foothill penstemon (*Penstemon heterophyllus*) provides showy, usually bright blue or purple flowers. Red-flowered buckwheat (*Eriogonum grande* var. *rubescens*) forms mounds of gray-green foliage under masses of pink flowers. Most penstemons and buckwheats do best with little water, or on hillsides, in raised beds, or with fast-draining soils.

Many of California's sages also fit well into a cottage garden. Mostly sun-loving, with aromatic leaves, sages bloom abundantly after the rainy season's end. Cleveland sage (*Salvia clevelandii*) and purple sage (*Salvia leucophylla*) are particularly garden friendly. Cleveland sage has bluish whorls of flowers, and its strong-scented leaves are said to be the best substitute for culinary sage. Purple sage is generally taller, with many clusters of pinkish blooms. A few less common sages, including creeping sage (*Salvia sonomensis*) and hummingbird sage (*Salvia spathacea*), tolerate light shade. Creeping sage, as its common name suggests, grows low to the ground, forming a wide gray-green carpet. Hummingbird sage has large leaves and vibrant spires of larger flowers, but don't rely on it by itself. It can get a bit ragged, even for the controlled chaos of a cottage garden. You might want it growing around a stalwart structural grass, like deer grass (*Muhlenbergia rigens*), if there's enough space.

For shadier spots in the cottage garden, good candidates include canyon sunflowers (*Venegasia carpesioides*), coral bells (*Heuchera*—there are many choices), and Pacific bleeding hearts (*Dicentra formosa*). Canyon sunflowers

Island morning glory climbs beside California wild grape. STEPHEN INGRAM

brighten up the shade with cheerful yellow blooms and light green leaves. They do best with regular water and hard pruning in the late summer. Coral bells are a familiar garden plant in and out of California. While some are diminutive enough to grow in the cracks of a garden's rock wall, others are over two feet high. Our native versions come in many varieties, with neat rounded mounds of foliage nearly one foot high and spikes of pink or white flowers. Pacific bleeding hearts are native to redwood forests. Their lovely pink flowers dangle sweetly from arching stems.

While the spirit of a cottage garden is the antithesis of rules, vines do seem to be de rigueur. Without question, the easiest long-blooming evergreen vine is the island morning glory (*Calystegia macrostegia*, a perennial, not the annual morning glory, *Ipomoea tricolor*, that might have attacked your childhood vegetable garden). If the garden contains an arbor, the morning glory can scramble up it and display its pale pink flowers. Along a picket fence, one might stagger a few plants at roughly ten- to fifteen-foot intervals. They may require cutting back every few years, but you can ensure that the fence will never be bare by cutting every other plant in alternate years. Other excellent flowering vines include pipestem clematis (or chaparral clematis, *Clematis lasiantha*) and virgin's bower (*Clematis ligusticifolia*). Both are deciduous and have somewhat fragrant cream-colored flowers in spring, followed by pretty puffy seed heads in fall. California wild grape (*Vitis californica*) is a robust climber with bold fall color.

Shrubs, rather than trees, seem to form the backbone, when there is one, of a cottage garden. Along with vines, they bring the garden up to eye level. The most coveted flowering shrubs for a cottage garden are ceanothus (*Ceanothus* spp.), flannel bush (*Fremontodendron californicum*), Matilija poppy (*Romneya coulteri*), pink-flowering currant (*Ribes sanguineum*), and wild mock orange (*Philadelphus lewisii*). The ceanothus is a fairly fast-growing evergreen with species in many sizes. It is worth growing for the foliage alone, but it is best known for its showy clusters of blue flowers in winter and spring. Flannel bush is a large shrub with fuzzy foliage and big, vibrant, yellow to gold flowers in spring and summer. (The fuzzy leaves may irritate your skin, so be careful pruning it.) It's another plant that ironically lives on in the English contingent of California plant ex-pats—

though it doesn't like the damp. It comes in many cultivars, including at least one developed in England, 'Tequila Sunrise'. The Matilija poppy can grow to eight feet in a single season and has flowers that look like a fried egg, sunny side up, and that are the size of a hand. It does well when cut back severely in fall, after its bloom is spent. It's a stunning plant with only one drawback: it's a notorious invader. So either keep it cordoned off or put it somewhere where there is ample room to grow. Consider it for a parking strip, where the neighbors can admire it but the rest of your garden will be safe.

The pink-flowering currant and the wild mock orange are good choices for light shade with moderate water. Both are deciduous. The pink-flowering currant is a somewhat upright shrub, often tall enough to peek over a fence. It is one of the earliest shrubs to flower, with pink clusters of blooms appearing as early as January. The mock orange is a similar height, but broader, with arching branches and white fragrant flowers that bloom in late spring or early summer.

Keep in mind that cottage gardens, native or not, are filled with vigorous growers and bloomers. This makes cutting them back and deadheading them the key chores. Cottage gardens have the casual look that allows some scope for messiness, but the vitality of the plants requires upkeep. Your work will be rewarded with the vibrancy and abundance that is the special charm of the cottage garden.

A JAPANESE GARDEN

The Japanese garden is at once the antithesis of both the formal garden and the cottage garden. Quiet and tranquil, a Japanese garden is a place of contemplation. It provides a retreat where one can reflect serenely on the subtle perfection of nature. Its design is a blend of simplicity and refined elegance, where nothing is showy and nothing is immediately revealed. All is symbolic, suggestive, and mysterious. Many elements contribute to the experience of a Japanese garden's serenity. One might glimpse the garden first from outside its gate, then enter by way of a path of aged, irregularly placed stepping stones. The path curves without symmetry, and its end remains unseen. At a bend in the path, we might find a view of water, or of carefully placed and buried rocks that evoke an island or distant mountain. The view is likely to be framed by sculpted, twisting trunks. All is trimmed carefully, emphasizing natural, asymmetric forms, and unfilled spaces are created. Color is delicate, sometimes even poignantly so. While we can't hope to re-create in a literal way the careful symbolism of a Japanese garden's most figurative plants, such as its pine, bamboo, and plum, the garden's other aesthetic qualities can inspire us, and we can reinterpret these qualities with California's own flora.

The reverence for age is embodied in a Japanese garden by the almost-bonsai pruning and twisted trunks of its evergreens. This feeling is evoked quite naturally by our own pines, such as beach pine and the rare Torrey pine (*Pinus contorta* var. *contorta* and *P. torreyana*), manzanita (*Arctostaphylos* spp.), madrone (*Arbutus menziesii*), and, on a larger scale, coast live oak (*Quercus agrifolia*) and Monterey cypress (*Cupressus macrocarpa*). The beach pine is an ideal bonsai specimen. As its Latin name suggests, its branches are contorted. Many manzanitas form shrubs or small trees with twisting, architectural branches. The madrone has a reputation of being difficult to grow, but it succeeds in many native gardens. Madrone depends on its microscopic partners under the soil's surface, so it may help if the plants arrive from the nursery with some native soil in their containers. It may also help if other natives are already established in the garden and not much watering is done over the summer. The coast live oak and the Monterey cypress also develop that gnarled branching habit, as long as they're not trimmed into lollipops at an early age.

California's junipers have an aged, windswept quality as well. These include the California juniper (*Juniperus californica*), Sierra juniper (*J. occidentalis*), and the tiny (and not so common) common juniper (*J. communis*). In the same spirit, though physically quite different, the California redwood (*Sequoia sempervirens*) inspires in many of us the same quiet reverence for age and nature that one feels in many Japanese gardens. This is particularly true when redwoods grow in groves of sufficient size and with modest underplantings.

The Japanese maple exemplifies the seasons' changes. In California, we might get the same feeling from a dogwood (*Cornus* spp.), a California hazelnut (*Corylus cornuta* var. *californica*), a vine maple (*Acer circinatum*), or—on a larger scale—a big-leaf maple (*Acer macrophyllum*). These are picturesque, deciduous, shrub-like trees that change gracefully from season to season. All of them naturally have a multi-trunked habit and provide a light canopy. Their leaves move with slight breezes, creating a dappled light. The dogwood is at home above three thousand feet and can be difficult to get started elsewhere; the hazelnut and the vine maple are more adaptable. The hazelnut grows in middle or lower elevations, and the vine maple occurs naturally along streams in the northern part of the state. The western redbud (*Cercis occidentalis*) is another multi-trunked, shrubby tree. In its case, however, its dense mass of pink blooms is its most notable feature (particularly where winter chill drops below 28° F.), and its flowers may stand in for the abundant small-petaled blooms of Japan's traditional cherry.

The camellias and azaleas of Japanese gardens are often pruned to look open and spare. Several of California's flowering shrubs, with their finely structured branching habits, fit this aesthetic well. Some good examples include the western azalea (*Rhododendron occidentale*), Pacific rhododendron (*Rhododendron macrophyllum*), and wild mock orange (*Philadelphus lewisii*). The pink-flowering currant also might fit in. Its foliage is delicate, and its pink flowers fall in graceful hanging clusters.

Small plants may accent a grouping of rocks or the base of a tree. Members of the horsetail family, such as scouring-rush (*Equisetum hyemale*) or giant horsetail (*E. arvense*), might provide verticality and a primitive feeling similar to that of bamboo. Ferns may peek out quietly from between rocks or at the base of a tree, as they would in nature. In shade, either giant chain fern (*Woodwardia fimbriata*) or swordfern (*Polystichum munitum*) could provide a large accent, and lady fern (*Athyrium filix-femina* var. *californicum*) or California polypody (*Polypodium californicum*) a smaller one. To mimic the setting of a rocky outcrop, lace fern (*Cheilanthes gracillima*) or Brewer's cliff-brake (*Pellaea breweri*) might work well.

Closer still to the ground, one may include a monochromatic, dark sweep of wild ginger (*Asarum caudatum,* which is not edible) in deep shade, or the more fine-featured kinnikinnick (*Arctostaphylos uva-ursi*) in light shade. A covering of native iris, such as Douglas iris (*Iris douglasiana*), will remain subtly green, except in spring, when beautiful—but never gaudy—

flowers will appear. Lower still, moss is the signature groundcover of a Japanese garden. It spreads from ground to rocks or a lantern, bestowing the venerable patina of age. In California, it can be encouraged to grow by keeping debris clear and adding water when it's needed.

A Japanese garden provides a quiet place for contemplation. Its serenity doesn't come from moss, stones, a lantern, or even a raked gravel bed. Nor does it come from bamboo, pine, or plum. It comes from the sensitive and subtle use of plants to express a reverence for nature. In this particular sense, an authentic Japanese garden outside Japan perhaps ought to use local flora. If what draws you to the Japanese garden is the precise blend of the picturesque and the exotic embodied in the bamboos and Japanese maples (and lanterns and bridges), then you will have to use some of the original Japanese plants and accoutrements. However, if its spirit and tranquility draw you in, then you have even more scope for interpretation with your own flora.

AN HERB GARDEN

At its simplest, an herb garden is merely a collection of plants that provide flavor, scent, or remedy. That collection can come in any form. Some of the most charming of these are patterned after the gardens of medieval monasteries. A medieval monastery's herb garden was characterized by orderliness. It typically existed within an enclosure, included raised beds, and had a central source of water. The orderliness of the medieval garden reflected its role as an early pharmacy. That orderliness still helps us sort herb from herb and herb from weed. An enclosure protects the tenderest plants and enhances the garden's aromas. Raised beds provide easy cultivation, easy gathering, and good drainage. Good drainage is important both to California's native herbs and to the familiar Mediterranean culinary herbs with which they grow so companionably. The raised beds also provide impromptu seating—often the best garden seating. Together, the orderliness, the enclosure, and the raised beds provide a structure that counterbalances the loose habits of most herbs. Finally, the medieval garden's central water source is handy and often beautiful.

Of course, there are many other models for the herb garden. Herbs are grown in containers on rooftops, in sunny suburban borders, in gravelly beds, and in clipped knot gardens. An herb garden is another great choice for an urban setting. Unlike many other garden styles, it is not the design that makes an herb garden an herb garden, it is the plants themselves. Like the Mediterranean, California is home to many aromatic, culinary, and beautiful herbs.

Many of California's most fragrant herbs thrive in sun. California bee balm (*Monardella undulata* var. *frutescens*) is our own rare version of bee balm, though more common relatives, such as coyote mint (*Monardella villosa*) and mountain monardella (*Monardella odoratissima,* also called western pennyroyal), would also be appropriate for a sunny spot in an herb garden. Woolly blue curls (*Trichostema lanatum*) is a pretty potpourri plant that blooms on and on through the year. Beach wormwood (*Artemisia pycnocephala*) is subtly fragrant and useful in dried flower arrangements. Yarrow (*Achillea millefolium*) is also a European herb. Its Latin name comes from the legend that Achilles's troops used it to treat their battle wounds (an early version of Betadine and a styptic pencil). Many other medicinal uses followed.

Some of California's more popular culinary herbs include chia (*Salvia columbaria*), Cleveland sage (*Salvia clevelandii*), miner's lettuce (*Claytonia* or *Montia perfoliata*), woodland strawberry (*Fragaria vesca*), yerba buena (*Satureja douglasii*), tule mint (*Mentha arvensis*), mountain violet (*Viola purpurea*), watercress (*Rorippa nasturtium-aquaticum*), and blue elderberry (*Sambucus mexicana*). You're probably familiar with chia sprouts growing in their own little ceramic garden on the back of someone's sink. The seeds from this small annual were toasted and eaten by many Native American tribes in California. Cleveland sage is fragrant, a long bloomer, and a substitute for culinary sage. In case you haven't tried miner's lettuce, it's like a fine, peppery butter lettuce. You might come across it in the woods near creeks, where it grows in spring, or in places where nasturtium (not a native) also volunteers. Herb gardens often incorporate berries, and you might consider California's woodland strawberry. It's a wonderful plant with delectable petite berries. It's easy to grow, will take some shade and water, has beautiful foliage, and displays pretty little white flowers. Yerba

Chia can grow with other dry-garden herbs. JUDY KRAMER

buena is said to make a good minty tea. It also makes an excellent mojito, with rum, lime, sugar, ice, and sparkling water, if you like. Tule mint, which requires some moisture, can be used like other mints. Mountain violet is both pretty and edible. Like others in the pansy clan, it can be added to salads or used to decorate cakes or pressed cheeses. Watercress can be grown if your herb garden includes a water feature. The fruits of the small elderberry tree are used for elderberry wine, as well as for jams and pies.

California has other berries that fit well in an herb garden or around it as a border. They include huckleberry (*Vaccinium ovatum*), western blueberry (*V. occidentale*), California blackberry (*Rubus ursinus*), thimbleberry (*R. parviflorus*), salmonberry (*R. spectabilis*), manzanita (*Arctostaphylos* spp.), and Oregon grape (*Berberis* spp.). Huckleberry is a northern California favorite. It provides delicious little berries on a well-mannered evergreen shrub. This beautiful plant grows near redwoods, so it's accustomed to moister and shadier conditions than many other herbs. It would fit nicely in the partly shaded end of an herb garden, and it would provide a visual backbone throughout the year. It grows well with tule mint and mountain violet. Huckleberry's cousin, western blueberry, is a bog plant, so it requires much more water. California blackberry grows well in sun and is drought tolerant. You might be afraid of blackberries because you've had experience with the *other* one, the monster nonnative Himalayan blackberry (*Rubus discolor*). That pest can expand its thorny thicket by as much as ten feet a year. Fear not, the California blackberry is a much nicer garden plant. It does have thorns, but they're small and straight (not huge, tough, and curved to catch you like the Himalayan's), and its canes, being round, are more flexible. It's a vigorous grower, but not a monster. You could tie its canes to a trellis at the back of the herb garden to lend some height and prune some of them back each year. Thimbleberry is somewhat smaller and has no thorns. It is very pretty, with edible red berries; but along with salmonberry, it requires regular water. Manzanita berries are said to be bland but full of vitamins and improved by cooking. Its leaves were once used in a salve to treat poison oak rash. The plants are evergreen and come in many forms; most of them are very drought tolerant. The low-growing forms drape well over the edges of raised beds, and the larger ones provide a nice garden backbone. Oregon grape is a common landscape plant. Its berries are used in cooking and are made into jelly and barberry wine.

Most herb gardens also contain some flowers. The California cousins of traditional herb garden flowers include California wild rose (*Rosa californica*), California mountain rose (*R. woodsii* var. *ultramontana*), blue dicks (*Dichelostemma capitatum*), and twinberry (*Lonicera involucrata*, also known as California honeysuckle).

Just have room for a couple of containers of herbs on a city rooftop? You might try combining yerba buena (*Satureja douglasii*) with mountain violet (*Viola purpurea*). Both can live in containers, and they can take the shady conditions that often face the urban gardener.

A CHILD'S GARDEN

What makes a garden attractive to children? Children don't want merely to look at a garden, unless, of course, something about it is quite strange. They want action. They want to touch, climb, pull, pick, plant, uncover, hide, and tromp. A fun plant is squishy, prickly, fuzzy, or tickly. When gardening themselves, most kids like something that grows fast and has obvious traits, like bright colors or big seeds.

They also like their own hideouts. A tepee is especially fun and can be made easily by training a vine to grow over long stakes tied at the top. With its evergreen cover and robust growth, island morning glory (*Calystegia macrostegia*) is as apt for a child's tepee as it is for a cottage garden's arbor. Its pale pink flowers are similar to those of the familiar morning glory (*Ipomoea tricolor*), which has poisonous seeds and is native to tropical areas in Central and South America. Two other fast-growing vines are deciduous: manroot (*Marah oreganus* and *M. fabaceus*, also called wild cucumber) and California wild grape (*Vitis californica*). As long as there is water, manroot grows fast. Between its large, slightly fuzzy leaves are twining tendrils that kids can tear off and lace through their fingers. Each seed pod is an otherworldly, gourd-like ovoid with prickly spines, a little like a rambutan. It's a bit weedy and it dies back during the dry season, but it might lend a longed-for "jungleness" to the right

Dutchman's pipe is the larval food for the pipevine swallowtail butterfly. RENATE KEMPF

child's garden. It also has a strange ball of a root that can grow as big as a man's head. Perhaps because of this strange root, it's rarely available from nurseries, but it can be grown from cuttings. Wild grape also grows fast. It is large and vigorous enough to cover the biggest tepee. The grapes themselves are edible, unlike the manroot seeds, which are poisonous. In fall, its leaves turn a lovely yellow or red color. In winter, the ropey vines invite a child's inventiveness, and the plant can take rough handling.

Another kid-friendly vine, but one that is less appropriate for the tepee, is Dutchman's pipe (*Aristolochia californica*). It is primitive and carnivorous looking. Its "pipes" are its flowers, which are pollinated by gnats that are trapped for a time inside. The plant is also the larval food for the pipevine swallowtail butterfly. It is said that in the right location, the swallowtail's caterpillars cover it so thickly that their munching becomes audible. Of course, a child might also be interested in an actual carnivorous plant, the cobra lily (*Darlingtonia californica*), if there's a nice wet spot for it. Children might also find butterflies in a large patch of one of our many buckwheats (*Eriogonum* spp.). Cliff buckwheat (*E. parvifolium*) suits south coast wildlife especially well. Coast buckwheat (*E. latifolium*) suits the coast from Monterey to Oregon, and its downy leaves are fun to touch. A five-foot by five-foot patch of buckwheat would probably be big enough for butterflies to find.

For brightness and for the gratification of growing flowers from seed, children can plant California poppies (*Eschscholzia californica*) and clarkias, such as farewell to spring (*Clarkia amoena*) and elegant clarkia (*C. unguiculata*). Both germinate reliably and grow quickly in spring. The poppies, of course, are orange or yellow. The clarkias can be red, pink, or white, and since they make excellent cut flowers, children can have the satisfaction of putting together their own home-grown bouquet for favored visitors. When the remaining flowers are finally spent and dry, children can stomp them down to encourage them to reseed (not that they need much encouragement).

There are also several flowering, easy-to-grow perennials that would be nice alongside a path. The most fairy-gardenesque among them is western columbine (*Aquilegia formosa*). Its preternatural, almost inside-out flowers are held on stems that arch several feet out over its clumps of delicate leaves. The sunrise colors of the flowers attract both hummingbirds and children. While western columbine is found in many parts of the state, it does best with regular moisture, sun in coastal areas, and shade inland. A sitting stone or log would bring children and adults to an excellent viewing height.

For a flowering groundcover, one might choose yarrow (*Achillea millefolium*) or California fuchsia (*Epilobium* spp.). Yarrow has bright green ferny foliage that can be mowed and walked on, and the California fuchsia has bright red or orange flowers that continue through late summer. Among flowering shrubs, a child might especially like bush monkeyflower (*Mimulus aurantiacus*), with its bright orange flowers and sticky leaves that can be picked off and stuck onto arms, legs, or foreheads for amusement. Or one might plant the more ragged but wildly beautiful hummingbird sage (*Salvia spathacea*), with its long spikes that support whorls of magenta flowers. The California fuchsia, the sticky monkeyflower, and the hummingbird sage together give another child's delight: a hummingbird garden from spring through early fall.

Among California's trees, many have special attributes to enchant a child. A favorite climbing tree is the coast live oak (*Quercus agrifolia*). Its low, twisting branches provide footholds and seats. A low horizontal limb can provide an impromptu balance beam. The live oak's only drawback is its prickly leaves: they're not barefoot friendly. Other native trees are interesting long before they are climbable. Even a young Catalina ironwood (*Lyonothamnus floribundus*) has peeling bark that children inevitably tear off in long strips. Its attractiveness is enhanced by its ferny, primitive leaves. Madrone (*Arbutus menziesii*) is also peelable, especially in summer, and the bark underneath is eerily smooth and cool. Instead of long strips, its bark peels into crisp, curved, paper-like sheets that can be drawn on with markers. The buckeye (*Aesculus californica*) has its own strangeness: "horse chestnuts." These large, pear-shaped fruits hang down from bare gray branches in fall. Under the fruit's leathery skin is a nearly baseball-sized glossy brown seed. In winter, the balls fall to the ground. Kids collect them "just because." While on paper they are poisonous, they are simply too big to try to eat. After the newness of collection wears away, they can be planted anywhere initially, even in a pail or an old toy truck. With any moisture, they will sprout on their own. You might pull some of them up, since they do have the drawback of being late-summer dormant. Once planted, they'll shoot up and form new leaves quickly.

If there's a feeling of wildness in a child's garden, it'll be filled with adventure. With a patch of some edible "wild" plants, a child becomes an imaginary native or a pioneer. Miner's lettuce (*Clatonia* or *Montia perfoliata*) will do, or woodland strawberry (*Fragaria vesca*), or thimbleberry (*Rubus parviflorus*) for a special sweet treat. If the garden attracts wildlife, then there's always something new and authentic to discover. A good wildlife garden shares a key ingredient with a good child's garden: a touch of abandon. Birds, insects, and lizards all benefit from a bit of leaf litter and brush for food and cover. A child benefits from a bit of leaf litter and brush for tromping, for imagining, and for uncovering treasures.

Cutting Times

The table below provides a rough guide for taking cuttings to propagate many familiar natives. The ideal timing varies from place to place and year to year. Use the table as a starting point for experimenting with cuttings of various genera in your own garden. (Keep in mind that taking cuttings on public land usually requires a permit.) For details on how to propagate your cuttings, see the discussion in November, pages 35–37. More details on some of the individual species are given in the monthly chapters.

OCTOBER	*Arctostaphylos*	*Erigeron*	*Rhamnus*
	Berberis	*Galvezia*	*Ribes*
	Ceanothus	*Heuchera*	*Salvia*

NOVEMBER	*Arctostaphylos*	*Garrya*	*Ribes*
	Berberis	*Heteromeles*	*Salvia*
	Ceanothus	*Heuchera*	*Symphoricarpos*
	Erigeron	*Lonicera*	*Vaccinium*
	Fremontodendron	*Rhamnus*	

DECEMBER	*Arctostaphylos*	*Fremontodendron*	*Rhamnus*
	Berberis	*Garrya*	*Ribes*
	Ceanothus	*Heuchera*	*Rubus*
	Cornus	*Heteromeles*	*Spiraea*
	Dudleya	*Philadelphus*	*Vaccinium*
	Erigeron		

JANUARY	Arctostaphylos	Erigeron	Heuchera
	Baccharis	Fremontodendron	Rhamnus
	Berberis	Galvezia	Salix
	Ceanothus	Garrya	Vaccinium
	Cornus	Heteromeles	Vitis
FEBRUARY	Arctostaphylos	Epilobium	Romneya
	Baccharis	Erigeron	Spiraea
	Berberis	Mimulus	Symphoricarpos
	Ceanothus	Philadelphus	Salvia
	Cornus	Rhamnus	
MARCH	Arctostaphylos	Epilobium	Mimulus
	Baccharis	Erigeron	Rhamnus
	Ceanothus	Heuchera	Salvia
APRIL	Arctostaphylos	Epilobium	Rhamnus
	Baccharis	Erigeron	Ribes
	Berberis	Lessingia	Salvia
	Ceanothus	Mimulus	Vitis
	Cornus	Myrica	
MAY	Baccaris	Erigeron	Salvia
	Carpenteria	Mimulus	Satureja
	Ceanothus	Philadelphus	Solidago
	Cornus	Rhamnus	Symphoricarpos
	Epilobium	Ribes	Vitis
JUNE	Ceanothus	Erigeron	Ribes
	Cornus	Philadelphus	Sambucus
JULY	Aristolochia	Ceanothus	Erigeron
AUGUST	Ceanothus	Erigeron	Ribes
SEPTEMBER	Arctostaphylos	Carpenteria	Erigeron
	Aristolochia	Ceanothus	Holodiscus
	Baccharis	Cercocarpus	Ribes
	Berberis		

Places to See Natives

There are many places throughout the state to see California's native plants in public gardens and in the wild. There are a few botanic gardens specializing in natives, and many more—including several university arboreta—with native collections. Several local nurseries and plant societies maintain demonstration gardens and host garden tours. The California Native Plant Society also welcomes the public on field trips to see native plants in their natural settings.

NATIVE BOTANIC GARDENS

Three botanic gardens stand out among the rest (listed from north to south): the Regional Parks Botanic Garden in Berkeley's Tilden Park, the Santa Barbara Botanic Garden, and the Rancho Santa Ana Botanic Garden in Claremont. Each of these large, venerable gardens is devoted exclusively to California's native plants, and they carry on a tradition of horticultural inquiry dating back to their early founders and directors. Dedicated to public education, they offer extensive display gardens and frequent classes and workshops throughout the year.

Regional Parks Botanic Garden
Wildcat Canyon Road and South Park Drive
Tilden Regional Park, Berkeley
(510) 544–3169
www.nativeplants.org

Santa Barbara Botanic Garden
212 Mission Canyon Road, Santa Barbara
(805) 682–4726
www.sbbg.org

Rancho Santa Ana Botanic Garden
1500 North College Avenue, Claremont
(909) 625–8767
www.rsabg.org

UNIVERSITY ARBORETA

Several university arboreta in the state include native collections. Some, most notably the extensive University of California Botanical Garden at Berkeley, made their start with California natives. Here, they are listed from north to south.

U.C. Davis Arboretum
La Rue Road, Davis
(530) 752–4880
http://arboretum.ucdavis.edu

U.C. Botanical Garden at Berkeley
200 Centennial Drive, Berkeley
(510) 643–2755
http://botanicalgarden.berkeley.edu

U.C. Santa Cruz Arboretum
Approximately 1490 High Street, Santa Cruz
(831) 427–2998
http://arboretum.ucsc.edu

Leaning Pine Arboretum
California Polytechnic State University
Via Carta, San Luis Obispo
(805) 756–2888
http://leaningpinearboretum.calpoly.edu

Cal State Northridge Botanic Garden
Lindley Avenue, Northridge
(818) 677–3496
www.csun.edu/botanicgarden

U.C. Riverside Botanic Gardens
Botanic Gardens Drive, Riverside
(951) 784–6962
http://gardens.ucr.edu

Fullerton Arboretum
1900 Associated Road, Fullerton
(657) 278–3407
http://fullertonarboretum.org

U.C. Irvine Arboretum
Campus Drive and Jamboree Road
North Campus, Irvine
(949) 824–5833
http://arboretum.bio.uci.edu

LOCAL BOTANIC GARDENS

Many local botanic gardens—large and small—include native collections. Some, such as the Wrigley Botanical Garden on Catalina Island, feature natives that are local to the area. Others, such as the spacious San Francisco Botanical Garden, include natives from throughout the state.

Dunsmuir Botanical Gardens
City Park, Dunsmuir
Dunsmuir Recreation District, (530) 235–4740
www.dunsmuirbotanicalgardens.org

Humboldt Botanical Gardens
North Entrance, College of the Redwoods
Highway 101, Eureka
www.hbgf.org/native.htm

Mendocino Coast Botanical Gardens
18220 North Highway 1, Fort Bragg
(707) 964–4352
www.gardenbythesea.org

San Francisco Botanical Garden at Strybing Arboretum
9th Avenue and Lincoln Way
Golden Gate Park, San Francisco
(415) 661–1316
www.sfbotanicalgarden.org

Descanso Gardens
1418 Descanso Drive, La Cañada Flintridge
(818) 949–4200
www.descansogardens.org

Conejo Valley Botanic Garden
350 West Gainsborough Road, Thousand Oaks
(805) 494–7630
http://conejogarden.org

Los Angeles County Arboretum and Botanic Garden
301 North Baldwin Avenue, Arcadia
(626) 821–3222
www.arboretum.org

Manhattan Beach Botanical Garden
Polliwog Park, Peck Avenue, Manhattan Beach
www.manhattanbeachbotanicalgarden.org

Wrigley Botanical Garden
Avalon Canyon Road, Avalon
Catalina Island
(310) 510–2595
www.catalina.com/memorial.html

San Diego Botanic Garden (formerly Quail Botanical Gardens)
230 Quail Gardens Drive, Encinitas
(760) 436–3036
www.sdbgarden.org

DEMONSTRATION GARDENS

Many local chapters of the California Native Plant Society maintain native demonstration gardens in various settings, including parks and schools, a cemetery (Sacramento), a library (Woodside), and a park in memory of Lester Rowntree and a beach garden (Monterey). Increasing numbers of local water districts and conservation districts also maintain gardens that include native plantings.

Several nurseries also have gardens. The demonstration grounds at Yerba Buena Nursery, on the San Francisco Peninsula, and the Theodore Payne Foundation, in Los Angeles, are extensive. Some nurseries, notably Las Pilitas Nursery in Santa Margarita, have test gardens where mature plants can be seen growing in difficult conditions.

Every year, more nurseries sell natives and show them in demonstration beds and gardens. The California Native Plant Society currently maintains a list of nurseries and other places to buy natives. The list (www.cnps.org/cnps/grownative/nurseries.php, at the time of writing) is organized by region and tells of on-site demonstration gardens. In addition, the California Native Plant Link Exchange provides an interactive website (www.cnplx.info) for selecting native plants and finding local nurseries that sell them.

Good Friends on the Bookshelf

NATIVE GARDENING IN CALIFORNIA

Bornstein, Carol, David Fross, and Bart O'Brien. *California Native Plants for the Garden.* Los Olivos, CA: Cachuma Press, 2005. 280 pages. An annotated listing of California's native plants suitable for the garden. Includes photos and detailed descriptions of cultural requirements. An outstanding reference.

Francis, Mark, and Andreas Reimann. *The California Landscape Garden: Ecology, Culture, and Design.* Berkeley: University of California Press, 1999. 254 pages. Habitat restoration and sustainable design mingle with details about California's plant communities, wildlife, and society.

Harlow, Nora, ed. *Plants and Landscapes for Summer-Dry Climates of the San Francisco Bay Region.* Oakland: East Bay Municipal Utility District, 2004. 320 pages. Includes photographs and descriptions of the use of many natives (and nonnatives). Useful throughout cismontane California.

Keator, Glenn, and Alrie Middlebrook. *Designing California Native Gardens: The Plant Community Approach to Artful, Ecological Gardens.* Berkeley: University of California Press, 2007. 352 pages. Native garden design structured around California's major plant communities. Includes sample plans with plant lists and gardening tips for each plant community.

Lowry, Judith Larner. *Gardening with a Wild Heart: Restoring California's Native Landscapes at Home.* Berkeley: University of California Press,

1999. 267 pages. Restoration gardening essays. Reflects much of what is at the core of the native gardening movement.

———. *The Landscaping Ideas of Jays: A Natural History of the Backyard Restoration Garden.* Berkeley: University of California Press, 2007. 292 pages. A celebration, a personal account, and a guide to backyard restoration gardening in California. Organized around California's "five" seasons. Builds on Lowry's earlier book, *Gardening with a Wild Heart.*

O'Brien, Bart, Betsey Landis, and Ellen Mackey. *Care and Maintenance of Southern California Native Plant Gardens.* Claremont, CA: Rancho Santa Ana Botanic Garden, California Native Plant Society, and Theodore Payne Foundation for Wild Flowers and Native Plants, 2006. 238 pages. Detailed descriptions of the care of popular Southern California natives. Includes an excellent discussion of pruning techniques, as well as of soil, watering, planting, and pests.

Rowntree, Lester. *Hardy Californians: A Woman's Life with Native Plants.* New, expanded edition. Berkeley: University of California Press, 2006. 391 pages. First published in 1936. A charming sketch of a time, a place, and a life focused on California's flora.

Schmidt, Marjorie. *Growing California Native Plants.* Berkeley: University of California Press, 1980. 400 pages. The classic introduction to the use of California's native plants in the garden. Thorough discussion of cultural requirements, including germination and propagation (which were crucial in its day, when there were few native nurseries).

Smith, Nevin M. *Native Treasures: Gardening with the Plants of California.* Berkeley: University of California Press, 2006. 288 pages. Personal appreciation of natives as a backdrop for sharing the author's rich horticultural expertise on some of California's best native garden plants.

SPECIALIZED BOOKS

Anderson, M. Kat. *Tending the Wild: Native American Knowledge and the Management of California's Natural Resources.* Berkeley: University of California Press, 2005. 526 pages. This hefty book describes the Native Americans' uses and culture of California's plants. It includes rich descriptions of traditional approaches to many gardening tasks, such as coppicing and other pruning, plant division, and seed harvesting.

Connelly, Kevin. *Gardener's Guide to California Wildflowers.* Sun Valley, CA: Theodore Payne Foundation for Wildflowers and Native Plants, 1991. 146 pages. In-depth descriptions of the habitat and garden uses of native wildflowers. Includes a thorough discussion of site preparation. Emphasizes Southern California, but useful for gardeners throughout the state.

Dubin, Margaret, and Sara-Larus Tolley. *Seaweed, Salmon, and Manzanita Cider: A California Indian Feast.* Berkeley, CA: Heydey Books, 2008. 122 pages. Covers the food of native Californians, including the culinary use of many of California's native plants.

Emery, Dara E. *Seed Propagation of Native California Plants.* Santa Barbara, CA: Santa Barbara Botanic Garden, 1988. 118 pages. This slim volume is a classic reference on growing California's native plants from seed.

Fross, David, and Dieter Wilken. *Ceanothus.* Portland, OR: Timber Press, 2006. 272 pages. A careful and detailed description of ceanothus species in the wild and in the garden. Includes many beautiful photos, descriptions of cultural requirements, and a selection guide.

Harlow, Nora, and Kristin Jakob, eds. *Wild Lilies, Irises, and Grasses: Gardening with California Monocots.* Berkeley: University of California Press, 2003. 274 pages. Photos, illustrations, and detailed descriptions of California's native monocots, their homes in the wild, and their garden uses and care. Particularly useful for its thoughtful and realistic discussions of lesser-known plants.

Keator, Glenn. *Complete Garden Guide to the Native Perennials of California.* San Francisco: Chronicle Books, 1990. 303 pages. Thoughtful discussions of native perennials and their uses in containers, borders, rock gardens, and more.

———. *Complete Garden Guide to the Native Shrubs of California.* San Francisco: Chronicle Books, 1994. 314 pages. Covers native shrubs and their care and includes the author's suggested uses. Complements his book on perennials.

Rowntree, Lester. *Flowering Shrubs of California and Their Value to the Gardener.* Stanford, CA: Stanford University Press, 1939. 317 pages. A lively and personal account of California's flowering shrubs, both in their native habitats and in the garden.

Acknowledgments

This book never would have been written without the members of the Santa Clara Valley Chapter of the California Native Plant Society, including Jeffrey Caldwell, Sally Casey, Melanie Cross, Ellie Gioumousis, Paul Heiple, Ken Himes, Don Mayall, Stephanie Morris, Steve O'Brien, Vicki Pelton, Georgia Stigall, Jean Struthers, Jim Sugai, Sharon Ward, and Wendy Winkler. Together, they planted the seed for the book more than a decade ago.

The idea made its way into a manuscript with the unwavering encouragement of Amy Kossow and with the early confidence of Jenny Wapner, who first took it up while she was still at the University of California Press. Dore Brown and Kate Marshall shepherded it from manuscript to book, and Jan Spauschus refined the text with sympathetic and intelligent copy editing. The contents also benefited from the knowledgeable review of Sarah Reichard, and that of Bart O'Brien, whose many insightful suggestions I could only begin to capture. Linda Chalker-Scott kindly shared some of her knowledge of plant respiration, and Douglas McCreary and Dieter Wilken provided invaluable insight into the links between field studies and home garden practices.

I also relied heavily on the comments and encouragement of Phyllis Anderson, Melanie Cross, Gerry Ellis, Diana Fleming, Kellogg Fleming, Ingrid Graeve, Leslie Gray, Michael Kevane, Anu Luther, Alrie Middlebrook, Ingrid Popper, and Scott Soden. Bill Sundstrom inspired me with well-worn Lester Rowntree editions, and Sharon Ward, there from the start, generously shared her bounty of seeds, cuttings, books, and wisdom.

Finally, I owe a debt to my husband and daughter, who encouraged me and gave me peace with the simple phrase "Mommy's writing."

Index

Page numbers in italics indicate photographs.

Frontis: California poppies. Photo by Helen Popper.

University of California Press, one of the most distinguished
university presses in the United States, enriches lives around
the world by advancing scholarship in the humanities, social
sciences, and natural sciences. Its activities are supported by
the UC Press Foundation and by philanthropic contributions
from individuals and institutions. For more information, visit
www.ucpress.edu.

University of California Press
Berkeley and Los Angeles, California

University of California Press, Ltd.
London, England

Designer and compositor: Claudia Smelser
Text: 10.5/15 Janson Pro
Display: Gotham
Indexer: Victoria Baker
Prepress: iocolor
Printer and binder: CS Graphics, Pte. Ltd.

LIBRARY OF CONGRESS CATALOGING-IN-PUBLICATION DATA

Popper, Helen Ann.
  California native gardening : a month-by-month guide /
Helen Popper.
    p. cm.
  Includes bibliographical references and index.
  ISBN 978-0-520-26534-9 (cloth : alk. paper)
  ISBN 978-0-520-26535-6 (pbk. : alk. paper)
  1. Native plant gardening—California. 2. Native plants for
cultivation—California. I. Title.
  SB439.24.C2P66 2012
  635.909794—dc23

                                              2011024486

Manufactured in Singapore

21 20 19 18 17 16 15 14 13 12
10 9 8 7 6 5 4 3 2 1

The paper used in this publication meets the minimum
requirements of ANSI/NISO Z39.48–1992 (R 1997) (*Permanence
of Paper*).